PRACTICAL PAINTED SCENERY: A GUIDEBOOK

JOE E. KEENER III

JK3 Publishing LLC

CONTENTS

Practical Painted Scenery:
  A Guidebook

Joe Keener III

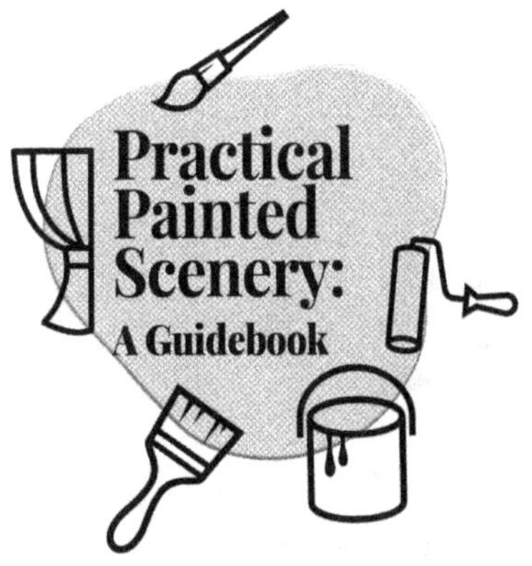

Cover design: Joe Keener III
Illustrations & Graphics: Elizabeth Nunnery & Joe Keener III
Editorial Assistant: Elizabeth Nunnery

"Art is a lie that makes us realize truth at least the truth that is given to us to understand. The artist must know the manner whereby to convince others of the truthfulness of his lies."

- Picasso

Practical Painted Scenery: A Guidebook

Joe Keener III

JK 3 Publishing LLC

PREFACE

The goal of this book, ***Practical Painted Scenery: A Guidebook*** is simple; to provide you, the reader/painter, with a concise and helpful reference to use while painting scenery for any theatrical production. At this point, I have been painting scenery for professional theater, television, film and theme parks for a long time (around 30 years, give or take), and teaching scenic painting for almost 10. This guidebook is intended to answer the 'big' questions for any painter in the most economical and practical way, with the aim of understanding that beautifully painted scenery can be created using simple tools and approaches and becomes 'beautiful' visually and achievable not through 'mysterious', sheer artistry but by layering simple steps with clear goals in mind. My hope here is to demystify scenic painting in a way and make it easy. I am still learning new approaches, materials and techniques for painting, many years into actively painting, studying and learning about the art and craft of scenic painting, but the goal is to give all the 'basics' here in this guidebook. Thanks for reading. Enjoy!

*For a more comprehensive look at scenic painting, look for my book on the subject: *Scenic Compendium: Techniques, Tools & Tricks for Theatrical Scenic Painting (with Emily Curtis)*. Publication 2023; JK3 Publishing, LLC.

Joe Keener III
    June 2023

Chapter 1
PLAN & PREP!

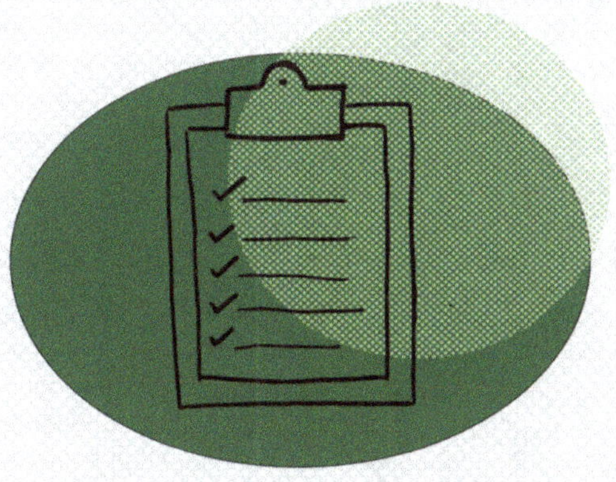

Planning & Preparation Makes For Better Painting

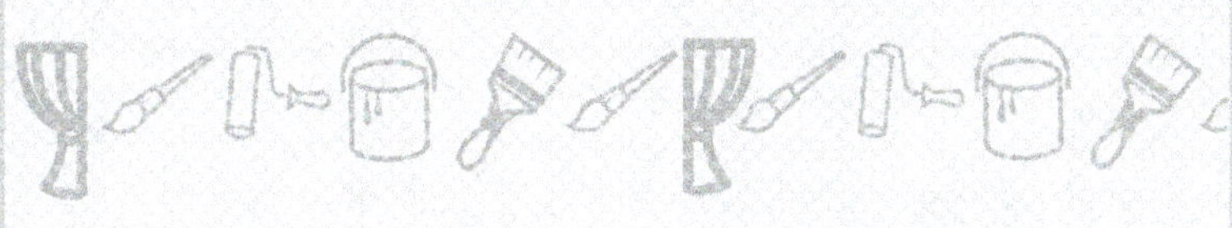

CHAPTER 1
PLAN & PREP!

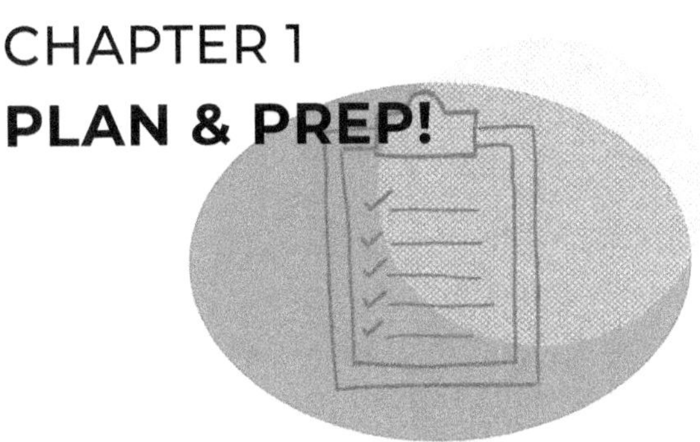

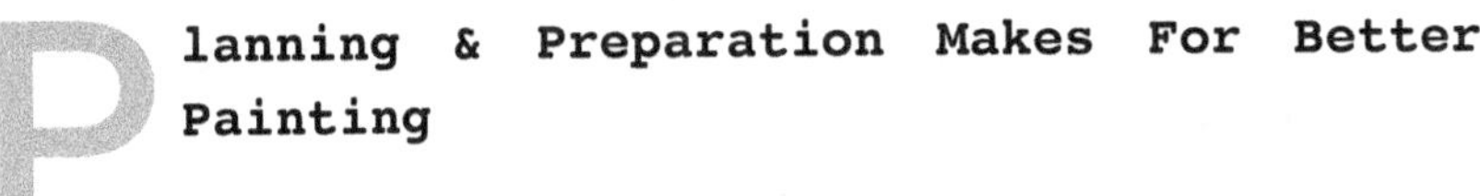

P lanning & Preparation Makes For Better Painting

IT IS ABSOLUTELY true that the look of any finished painting project largely depends on the planning and the preparation that came before it. Step **one** in the entire process, of course, is to review all of the scenic designer's final plans (known as *'paint elevations'*), ask any questions that you might have in order to clarify the designer's visual intent, and speak to the scenic designer to gain a clearer sense of the look, feel, and aesthetic direction of the painted scenery. I have found that, in talking with the scenic designer and reviewing the paint elevations, certain key stylistic words and aesthetic 'mood' preferences often become crystallized. Proceed with proper paint planning from there.

Often, when working on paint jobs for theatrical scenery, tight painting deadlines may require that some short-cuts and skipped steps are taken during the painting process - but it depends on the general standards of a particular paint shop or a particular charge painter. I always recommend taking a little bit of extra time up front to plan and to do proper 'prep' steps. Here are some key things to consider when planning a paint job and preparing the material surfaces (or 'substrates') to be finished.

Planning

1. **LOOK AT THE BUDGET**- simply put, you can only purchase as much paint and painting supplies (not to mention the cost of labor to pay additional painters to work on the job at hand) as the allotted paint budget will allow. Spend a bit of time assessing how much paint and supplies you will need to do a job and plan accordingly. Decide which tools and paint materials are absolutely necessary for the job.
2. **ESTIMATE FOR MATERIALS**- take a look at how much paint will need to be purchased based on adding up the total amount of square feet that all of the scenery requires. Estimate for enough material to do each of the following steps: priming, texturing/coating, base painting, adding other colors as painted layers of any type, clear coat finishes, and any flame-treating materials needed. Account for 5-10% of extra material as wasted paint or paint needed for touch up work down the road.
3. **WORK OUT A SCHEDULE**- work out a general timeframe or schedule in which all painting tasks that will be needed can take place. Some consideration will be needed, for example - scheduling the painting of a backdrop (drop) or a painted show deck (a painted floor comprised of sheet goods of 4x8 masonite or other material) to happen first on a schedule, often while other, more time-consuming/ carpentry-intensive building of scenery takes place. Don't underestimate how long something will actually take to prepare a surface, shop or

a piece of scenery to be painted, including all necessary steps, some trial and error along the way, and dry time in between coats of paint.

4. **PURCHASE PAINTS**- purchasing high quality paints and painting supplies will actually 'save' money in the end. A good rule of thumb is to never buy the cheapest paint product or supply as it will either function poorly or break, and that buying the most expensive paint product is generally not necessary on a theater set, since it does not need to last for a long period of time. Sticking with 'high' or 'good' quality materials, typically made for interior applications, will serve you well overall. Some exceptions can be considered if added washability or extra durability is required.

5. **ASSIGN TASKS**- while assigning, or delegating, painting tasks to separate painters, consider utilizing the strengths and skillsets of each. Also, consider the usefulness of working with a painter that has a great curiosity or eagerness to learn something new, as this can often be really productive and energizing during the painting process. On a daily basis, it is typically best to spend the first part of the work day on the 'hardest' task - like texturing, priming, filling, even shop cleaning and set up tasks so that the second part of the work day can be dedicated to often slower, or more artistically demanding processes. Remember also that the 'end' of each work/painting shift should be spent cleaning brushes, tools and organizing painting materials; making sure that all paint containers, sprayers, roller trays are closed and/or sealed overnight.

PREPARATION

1. **CLEAN**- sometimes overlooked, it is always a great idea to spend some time cleaning a piece of scenery before it can be prepped and painted. Use a piece of 180 grit sandpaper or a sanding 'sponge' (sandpaper sponge) to remove slightly rough cut edges on a piece of built scenery; Use a vacuum to remove extra sawdust. Sweep the floor closest to the painting area and the general work area. A large, lightly dampened 'flat' sponge, known as a 'car and boat' sponge, is useful to remove fine dust from a surface. A flat 'microfiber' mop is great for damp-mopping hard masonite, or other, sheet goods just before priming.

2. **SET UP**- take a little bit of time to sweep the floor, lay down a layer of brown 'Kraft' paper and masking tape/ plastic sheeting/ or a painter's drop cloth underneath the piece of scenery that needs to be prepped and painted. Setting a 'hard' piece of scenery (like a platform, a wall unit, or step unit for example) 'up' on blocks (scrap pieces of 2x4s or 1x material) can help make painting faster and cleaner, with less chance of painted scenery 'sticking' to the surface it was painted on; and less chance of 'picking up' dirt or debris from the floor and transferring it on to painted scenery. Setting up smaller pieces that need to be painted on sawhorses connected by long, flat boards or 'runners,' or on the surface of a table can also help speed up the overall production of painting. Consider also using blocks or cut 'sticks' of wood that are covered with a piece of wax paper or masking tape to keep things clean.

3. **FILL HOLES**- many 'theater' paint shops do not make a habit of filling nail holes, screw-holes, or other surface imperfections left by carpentry or assembly, but generally

speaking 'filling holes' will always make your painted scenery look better and more professional in the end. There are several different types of products available for filling tasks, but I am including only what I consider to be the truly 'essential' filling products here, along with a brief description of what their uses might be: *spackle* (usually includes a vinyl or flexible component; useful for general filling of small nail or screw holes and sometimes narrow gaps or cracks. Keep in mind that spackle is useful but expensive by volume). *joint compound* (sometimes called 'ready-mixed' joint compound, this is the most inexpensive and widely used filler). Best used for 'skim-coating' entire (wall or vertical) surfaces that require an overall smoother appearance after painting; for quickly filling small nail and screw holes - with the understanding that the material will most likely shrink a bit as it dries, requiring it to be sanded or filled with a second pass later; in combination with paper tape or fiberglass mesh tape to tape and 'bed' seams on walls; as a 'staple' ingredient to be used when thickening paint or mixing a 'universal' texture coating material, such as a scenic 'dope/roping' mix - a mix of joint compound, paint or primer, and white glue; *plaster* ('plaster of Paris' is what is typically thought of as a 'plaster' and it can certainly be a useful filling material to keep on hand, but the 'best' so-called plaster to keep on hand is sheetrock/joint compound powder). Although it is not referred to as 'plaster' per se, this product is technically a plaster since it generates a chemical/heat reaction after adding water and mixing thoroughly; it is, I think, the best overall product to use for quickly filling holes - including relatively 'deep' holes and seams on scenery - since it dries more quickly than joint compound and does not shrink, unlike joint compound which dries through evaporation; *wood filler* (can be 'latex' wood filler, or powdered wood filler, usually water based/ water cleanup) can be a tough, fast solution for the occasional nail hole and useful because it does not shrink much when drying - although somewhat expensive; *acrylic latex caulk* (generally referred to as 'painter's caulk') is a must-have product, since it is water-based, paintable, flexible and great for gaps smaller than one-eighth of an inch or so, and can often be used to fill small 'pin nail' holes and imperfections and is also a handy adhesive for small, decorative items. Best to purchase '20-minute' dry time/ paint-ready caulk, which is the fastest widely available.

4. **PRIME**- using some type of 'primer' coating before applying so-called 'base' paint (or 'lay-in' paint), or even before applying an overall texture coating can be an invaluable first step after the filling and 'bodywork' phase. Depending on the material (or substrate) to be painted, scene shops usually start with a coat of an interior grade water-based latex or acrylic-latex primer, though often will simply use a coat of interior grade flat white latex 'house' paint as a 'primer' coat to save a few dollars. It's worth noting that using an interior/exterior grade acrylic ('bonding') primer can be well worth spending a few more dollars per gallon to purchase when it comes time to prime any sheet good material that will be used for a painted 'show' flooring, since these types of primers inherently have the highest degree of adhesion. See Chapter 2 for more specific information about what types of primers and paint products to use on different surfaces. Also, consider tinting your primer 'toward' the top-coat/ 'base' paint color (for example, when painting a blue 'top-coat' or 'base paint,' add a bit of blue paint or universal tint/colorant to the primer to shift it slightly away from white to pale blue). Often, starting with a gray primer works better as a 'universal' primer coat than a

white primer. If the overall success of a finished paint job requires the look and feel of a 'watercolor' painting, or light and saturated colors applied thinly then starting with white is best.

5. **COAT OR TEXTURE OPTION**- depending on the look and feel required by the design of the finished, painted scenery, it may be helpful or necessary to apply a thicker coating or applied texture at this stage - before working with color(s). There are numerous custom textures and specialty products available for a painter to utilize, but keeping a few 'staple' products around to mix in various ratios for different applications generally works well. The most useful materials to have on hand, always, are: white glue (a pva glue, not so-called 'school glue'), joint compound, setting-type joint compound powder (a plaster), elastomeric 100% acrylic roof coating, powdered base coat plaster. By altering the combinations and quantities of each of these 'staple' materials when mixing up batches of coating or texture for scenery, a painter has a great degree of control over the best option or 'formula' for a range of different 'looks' and applications; from thin to thick, from smooth to aggressive texture. Chapter 2 will look closer at different options.

Chapter 2
CHOOSE WISELY!

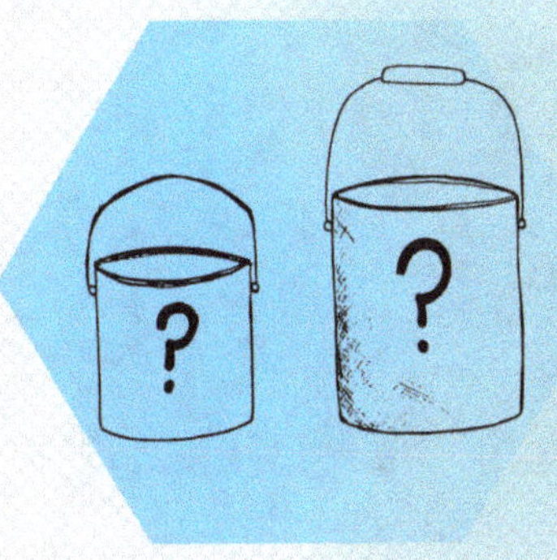

Paint & Materials Basics

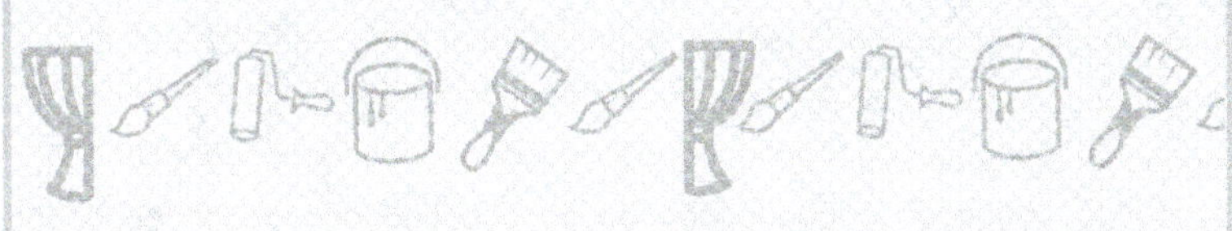

CHAPTER 2
CHOOSE WISELY!

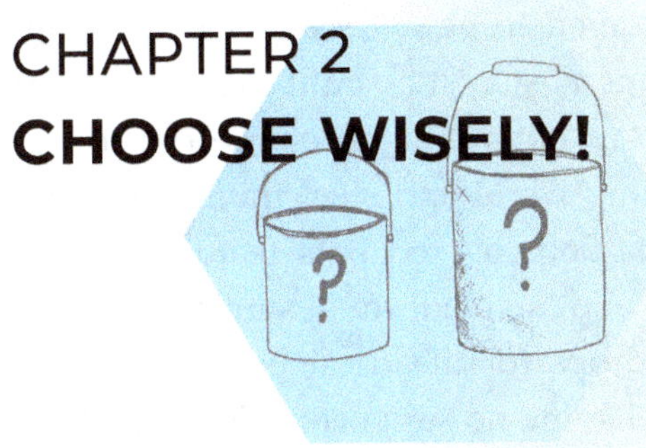

P aint and Materials Basics

HAVING a basic understanding of the range of different paints and supporting painting materials that are available, and knowing what these different products are made to 'do' will go a long way in helping you select the best paint products for your production.

HOW TO CHOOSE?

IN ORDER TO determine the most appropriate painting product(s) to purchase and use, it is best to think about what the scenery is made of first and foremost, and how is the scenery to be used in performance. Think of this as the *'form'* - the aesthetics, or the look - and the *'function'* - the utility, or practical considerations - of the scenery. All paint & material choices will be tailored to suit both the form *and* the function. More often than not, scenery that has been constructed specifically to be used 'on stage' in a theater as theatrical scenery will fall into two broad categories: 'hard' and 'soft' scenic elements. That is, scenic elements built mostly out of wood are considered to be *hard* scenic elements and those made mostly out of fabric are considered to be *soft* scenic elements. By extension, hard-covered flats are mostly 'stick-built' wooden (pine) framing with a covering (a 'skin') of wood paneling or sheeting. Platforming and stairs, including wood and steel frame construction, are hard scenic elements. Soft-covered flats feature fabric - muslin typically - stretched and stapled to a similar wooden stretcher frame. Painted backdrops for theatrical productions are soft scenic elements, generally having no supporting frame, but are hung from a batten pipe from above and weighted with a pipe inserted into a pipe pocket sewn along the bottom edge of the backdrop.

I am including a helpful table below that can be utilized when selecting the appropriate primer and/or paint product and matching it to a specific material surface ('substrate'). A few odd but sometimes used materials have also been included here. Assume that all products indicated are 'waterborne' paint products, otherwise known as 'water-based' products that clean up easily with water and soap. I recommend using Murphy's Oil Soap diluted with water at a ratio of approximately (1:8 soap:water) for cleanup, instead of regular 'dish' soap.

Material to be Painted	Form/function	Primer	Paint ('top') coating
1. Wood paneling, such as lauan	Hard covered flat/ decorative	Flat white interior grade latex or water-based latex primer	Interior grade, flat sheen theatrical paint - *Rosco* brand or flat sheen interior grade latex 'house' paint
2. Wood panel/ hardboard sheet-good	Painted flooring, or 'show' decking/ decorative	Acrylic-latex interior grade, or interior/ exterior grade water-based primer	Eggshell sheen interior grade 'house' paint - purchase at a 'big box' or 'hardware' store, or other paint provider
3. Plywood	In less than perfect grade, including platforming and step tread surfaces	White latex primer or paint thickened with ready-mixed joint compound, or elastomeric acrylic roof coating	Eggshell interior paint, satin sheen or higher sheen paint. Or, flat theatrical paint followed by a clear sealer (polyurethane)
4. Steel	Mostly structural, sometimes decorative	Clean metal first with a degreaser, liquid *Lysol* works well; prime with acrylic interior/ exterior 'bonding' primer	Any 'house' paint coating, or theatrical paint coating. Or, use an acrylic 'DTM' - direct-to-metal - paint in a solid color, skipping a primer coat
5. Muslin fabric	Opaque paint treatment/ decorative	Thinned flat white interior latex with white glue added (ratio of 1:2-1/2:1/2 paint:water:glue); or acrylic latex primer thinned with water. 2 coats sprayed; first coat is thinner than 2nd	Flat, eggshell latex or theatrical paint reduced with water - at ratio of 1:1-1/2 (paint: water), apply 2 coats for spray application. For brushing, mix at a ratio of up to 4:1 (paint: water)

Material to be painted	Form/function	Primer	Paint ('top') coating
6. Muslin fabric	Translucent paint treatment/ decorative	Prime (size) with *Argo gloss* laundry starch first; or 'clear' size/prime with clear acrylic flat; or apply several very thin coats of white glue/water	Assuming translucent look, apply highly reduced (1:20, paint: water) watercolor sprays or washes with a large brush
7. PVC, plastic, fiberglass	opaque coating treatment	Wipe surface first with isopropyl (rubbing) alcohol, then light scuff sanding, 2nd wipe; prime with acrylic bonding primer	Any high quality acrylic paint, or theatrical paint should work well; eggshell, satin sheen recommended
8. plexiglas	Translucent paint treatment/ decorative	Wipe surface first with water, clean with a microfiber cloth; prime surface with clear semi-gloss or satin acrylic polyurethane	Apply acrylic paint, artist's grade for color; thin material with small amounts of water and clear acrylic polyurethane
9. Foam	Decorative paint and/or texture coating	Mix latex paint with joint compound and white glue; or mix joint compound and elastomeric acrylic roof coating	Any flat latex or acrylic paint coating will work; consider spray application using a hopper gun or thick-nap roller cover

Chapter 3
TOOL TIPS!

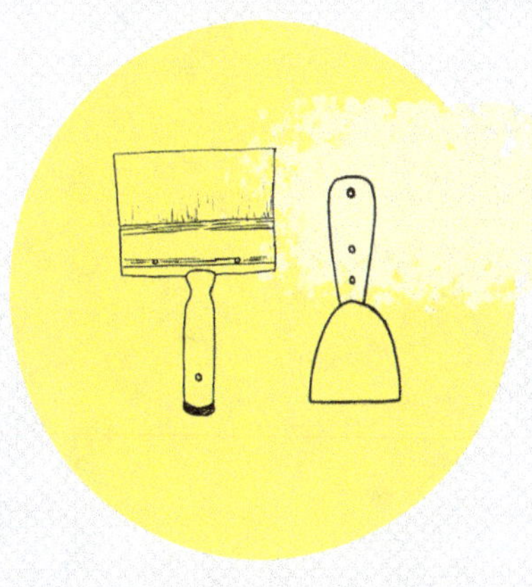

Basic Painting Tools Are Best

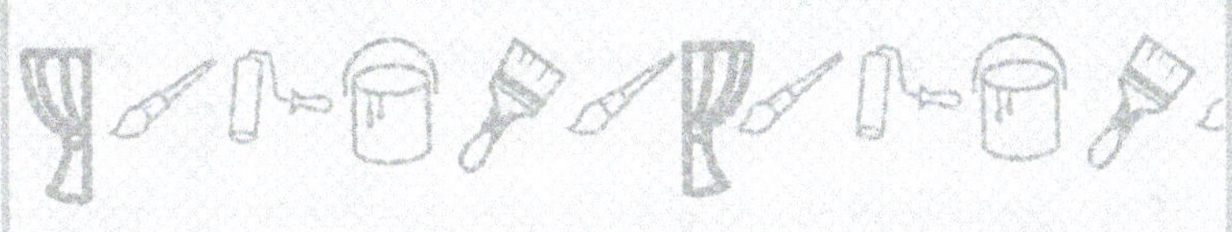

CHAPTER 3
TOOL TIPS!

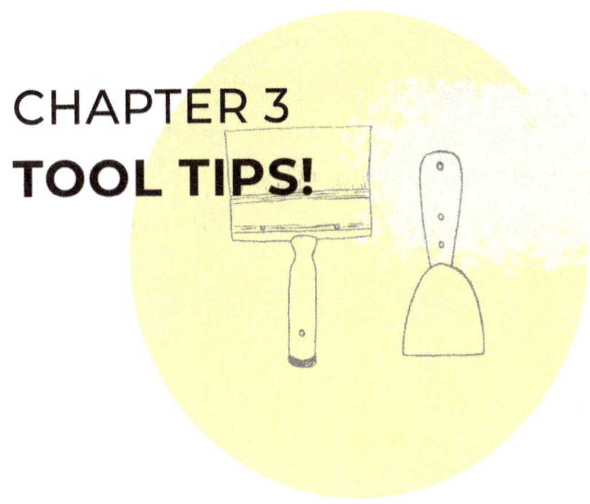

Basic Painting Tools Are Best

Since the main goal of this guidebook for the scenic painter is to provide practical painting tips that can be used for painting 'successful' theatrical scenery (both technically and artistically), it is important to emphasize the use of widely available painting tools over the use of more specialized - read, *more expensive* - tools marketed for a 'fine' artist's use.

Unless there is an 'artist's grade' brush or painting tool that is unlikely to be replaced with a more commonly available, more inexpensive painting brush or tool, such as those found at most big box hardware and paint supply stores - a fan brush or a sword-striping brush are good examples - I find it really useful to approach the selection and daily use of painting tools by purchasing, and often modifying, readily available tools in quantity. This practice proves much more useful, considering there are typically several painters working on a set at the same time and each of them may need the same painting tool. I will mention the general types of painting brushes and tools - and suggest ways to modify ('pre-pare') them here.

For most painting tools, indeed most tools in general, there are always options or grades available to buy. Think of them as 'good,' 'better,' and 'best.' Most of the time, it is not really necessary to purchase the most expensive, 'best' grade, tool and usually not very practical to purchase the cheapest one either. Aim for 'better' in terms of quality and construction. The same is usually true when buying 'house' paint as well.

The Essential Painting Tools

These are the 'Essential' painting tools/brushes/equipment to have on hand for scenic painting:

1. **Fitch brushes** - long handled, round, natural bristle brushes common in theatrical scenic painting. Good for lining, washes, and scumbles.
2. **Large lay-in brushes** - usually 4, 5 or 6-inch wide, flat bristle brushes that feature a removable, 'screw' handle. These are often called 'deck and fence' painting brushes, and are often used at the end of an extension pole.
3. **Extension pole(s)** - wooden or metal poles for extending the reach of a wide paint brush, featuring a metal thread at one end. Used in 'continental-style' painting technique; that is, the painter stands and paints with the scenery laid flat on the floor. Common drop painting, flat painting watercolor wash and floor painting uses.
4. **Bamboo pole(s)** - length of bamboo with several linear cuts made at one end, most often used for extending the painting reach of a long handled paintbrush like a scenic fitch or sash (angle) brush. Brush is held in place using a thick rubber band or elastic hair tie. Can be

purchased at gardening supply stores and fishing supply stores.

5. **Chip brushes** - inexpensive, flat natural bristle 'economy'/utility paint brushes. These feature a flat wooden handle. Best to keep the following sizes: 1, 2 and 4 inch. The 4 inch chip brush is ubiquitous for use in painting faux woodgrain (by modifying, cutting out random 'fingers' across the bristles with a pair of scissors) as a *'finger-hair' graining* tool and commonly used for applying texture and aging glazes.

6. **Paint rollers** - standard 'house' painting roller frames and roller covers (and roller trays) are a staple of a paint shop. The common size is a 9-inch wide roller and the most common roller nap is 3/8ths of an inch thick (used for most priming and base-painting applications), but having a 3/4 inch nap or 1 inch nap roller is great for *'back-rolling'* (softening sprays and aging washes). Other rollers are 18-inch wide, for quick painting of sheet goods, decks, walls; and 4-inch and 6-inch wide fabric covered *'whizz'* rollers that can be great for railings, trim, facings, and many scenic painting effects.

7. **'House' painting brushes** - This is a generic term for any synthetic bristle (nylon, polyester) paint brushes. Best used for thick, even applications of acrylic paints and opaque 'base' painting. Also, great for even application of clear acrylic polyurethane sealer on doors and other surfaces.

8. **Paint buckets** - having a couple sizes of containers and some lids for mixing, storing and working (*'work-pails'* or *'cut-buckets'*) is always necessary. Most often, painters will need the following sizes: 1 quart, 2-1/2 quart, 5 quart with handles - as work-pails, and 5 gallon buckets - for use with a roller grid and roller frame, supplying water while painting washes, and for storing mixed textures, primer and paint color.

9. **5-in-1 'Painter's Tool'** - the most commonly used tool in most paint shops. Used for opening, and sealing paint cans as well as scraping, applying spackle or other filler to nail and screw holes and cleaning roller covers with the 'half moon' contour.

10. **Mixing sticks** - wooden sticks used for stirring and mixing paint materials, available in one gallon and five gallon length sizes.

11. **Sprayers** - theatrical scenic painters often rely on hand-held, 'small' and larger capacity 'tank' sprayers for applying diluted paint washes, spatters, and 'aging' sprays on scenery. These sprayers are most often made for gardening and chemical spray uses. Commonly used in a paint shop are small 'spray bottles,' medium-sized hand-held 'half-gallon' (48-ounce actual capacity) *'floretta'* (*'Chapin'*) sprayers, 'one-gallon' lawn/bug sprayers - featuring a spray wand and short length of hose - ideal for most spatters and sprays, and larger *'Hudson'* type tank sprayers, often 2-1/2 gallon capacity - used when spraying larger amounts of water, liquid sizing, and flame-treating saturant solutions on backdrops and soft covered scenery.

12. **Sponges & rags** - organic, 'sea' sponges are often used to paint interesting textures, such as faux rust and stone. Large, flat, rectangular *'car and boat'* sponges are used for wiping on thinned paints and glazes and wiping away excess material on surfaces with some low relief or carving details, leaving darker 'age' behind in the recesses. In addition, the use of medium nap texture 'Terry' cloth rags and cheesecloth are great applicators of thinned layers of color and glaze where visual movement and layers of subtlety are important.

13. **Tape** - 2-inch contractor's grade 'masking' tape, and blue painter's tape are commonly used while painting; for securing masking paper and other materials to a

paint shop deck ('*masking*' tape), and for creating sharply painted lines on finished scenery (blue '*painter's*' tape).

14. **Staple gun** - hand held staple guns are most often used, with 3/8th inch or 1/2 inch staples, to secure muslin fabric to flats and stretcher frames, and for tacking large backdrops to a wooden paint shop deck floor to prepare the theatrical backdrop for painting.

15. **Mops & brooms** - In addition for the necessary paint shop floor sweeping upkeep, done on a daily basis and prior to any deck preparation for a painted backdrop, large push brooms and smaller brooms/dustpans are must have items. Brooms have other uses while painting traditional 'spatter and drag' graining techniques for quick wood grain looks on decking and for combing textures. A microfiber (flat) mop is great for cleaning and prepping hard covered flats and sheet goods before painting begins, and can also be used for quick applications of soft 'wood' grain looks along with glazes and washes and many other quick, broad wet scumbled looks.

16. **Trash bags** - Paint shops, all shops, need large plastic trash bags for cleanup and maintenance purposes, and plastic trash bags may also be very useful for cutting apart and creating 'organic' textured glazes - as the basis of interesting 'marble' structure painting processes; as well as temporary lining a paint roller tray for clean paint application and quick clean up. Can also keep paint tools from drying out when waiting for second coat/ recoat times.

17. **Squeegees** - small, hand-held, rubber edges squeegees and large scale floor squeegees are useful for custom creating random 'v'-notched texture, strié, and grain combing tools. Large squeegees can form a great foundation over which to wrap cheesecloth and other

fabrics to quickly create large scale softened, varied faux wood looks.

18. **Trowels & putty knives** - Any scenic wall flat or surface in need of a typical troweled 'plaster' finish or 'knockdown' texture finish will be possible by using a large hand-held drywall finisher's or mason's trowel (10-14 inch sizes work well generally). Ready mixed joint compound, with some paint color - with or without some glue - added will create believable faux plaster textures, while applying 2 or more tinted textures or thickened paint colors with a trowel as a sort of 'all-over' troweled scumble process will produce a visually interesting 'Venetian' plaster-like, or faux concrete look. Paint itself may be thickened by adding powdered plaster and/or powdered joint compounds as well as by adding in clear wallpaper paste which can thicken paint slightly without altering the color. Putty knives are needed for filling holes left behind by screws, staples or nails.

19. **Paint colors & clear coats** - of course, all paint shops need at least a 'basic' selection of standard paint colors (the primary colors of red, yellow, blue; and basic set of 'earth' tone colors) and clear coat finishes, used to make glazes and for protective sealing of finished, painted scenery. Clear vinyl-acrylic binder clear flat is most often used for mixing translucent glazes on scenery; while waterborne acrylic polyurethanes in satin or semi-gloss sheens are most useful to seal and toughen painted flooring materials. Larger amounts of flat white and black paint and primer are typical in a paint shop.

20. **Filling compounds & caulk** - the last category on the list, but certainly not the least, is the inclusion of filling compounds, such as ready-mixed joint compound and spackle. In general, joint compound in both ready-mixed and in powder form (for faster filling of thicker, deeper imperfections) is the way to go. Spackle materials, while

certainly useful, are much more expensive by volume. Latex and acrylic latex ('house-painter's') caulk is extremely useful for quick filling of small staple holes and for seam filling that can be minimally applied, flexible, paintable, and sets up quickly - recommend buying 'fast' dry caulk.

Chapter 4
CUT & ROLL!

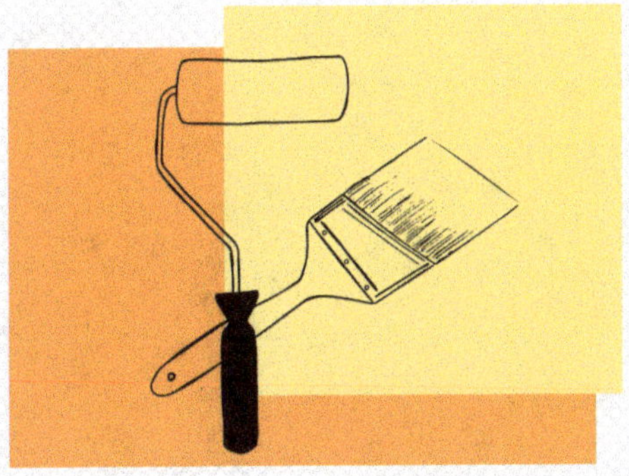

Brush & Roller Basics

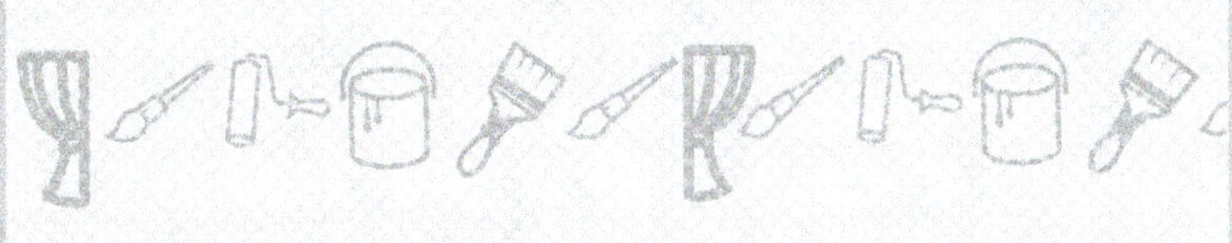

CHAPTER 4
CUT & ROLL!

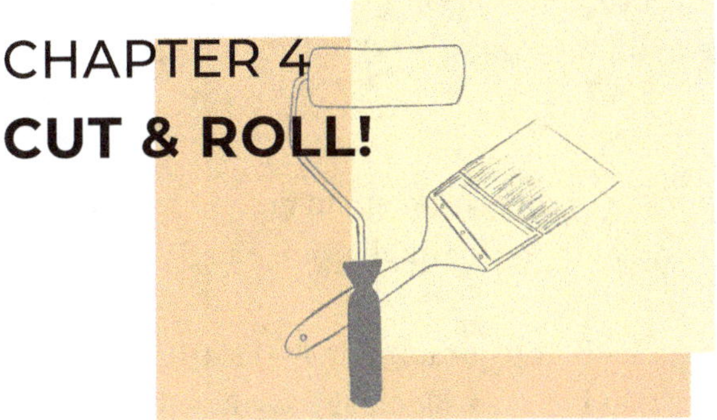

B rush and Roller Basics

WITHOUT QUESTION, the two most fundamental painting tools - or tool categories - that a set painter relies upon for the majority of daily painting tasks are the *paint brush* and the *paint roller*. Since these two categories include a wide range of options available to the painter, this section is all about mentioning the most important options and the most basic and useful thoughts about each category.

One of the most dependable concepts about the 'correct' painting technique when using a brush and roller is the following truism: *First cut, then roll.* That is, a skilled painter will always 'cut in' the clean edging, along the floor, along the baseboard trim, in the corners of a room or a set, etc, with a paint brush first, while leaving about 2 to 3 inches of brush work behind followed quickly by 'rolling' the remaining wall surface, or 'field,' with a paint roller second. Cut, then roll.

Cutting and rolling is typically done using a 2 or 3 inch 'house-painter's' (nylon or polyester synthetic bristle) paint brush; most often a flat lay-in type or angled, 'edging' or 'sash' brush to do the cut work. This is quickly followed up with a standard 9-inch, 3/8th or 1/2 inch nap (smooth) roller cover and roller frame/ roller tray setup and a roller pole to do the rolling work.

HERE ARE a few important things to keep in mind, the general painting 'rules' to follow that make for quality finishing:

1. **Clean, prep & mask** - Before jumping in and starting to paint, it is always good to take a look at the current condition of the wall(s) and other surfaces that you are preparing to paint. Proper prep work cannot be over-stressed. Start by wiping down and cleaning any surface containing dirt, oil, grease, or dust. Use a bucket of warm water and cleaning product - like liquid *Lysol*, *Windex*, white vinegar or a liquid tri-sodium phosphate or comparable solution - first to clean off any grease, oil, fingerprints. A microfiber cloth or paper towels are fine. Remove any dust or dirt with a vacuum cleaner. Prep the floor with a long 'runner' type drop cloth, mask off the top edge of door frames and baseboards with painter's tape, remove any existing nails or light switch plate covers, etc, from surface to be painted. Have a short ladder on hand.

2. **Patch & fill** - If there are minor surface imperfections and/or nail holes in the wall, use a ready mixed vinyl spackle to fill, or use joint compound, or mix up a small amount of plaster or powdered compound to use on deeper holes. Joint compound is not really appropriate for deep holes, anything much deeper than 1/8th of an inch. Painter's caulk may be used for cracks and small gaps. If there are 'large' holes in a surface that require attention, use fiberglass mesh tape first to cover the hole,

then apply a couple of passes of plaster, sanding lightly after each pass has dried. Using 'medium' mesh (180 grit) sandpaper typically works well. Remove any dust before proceeding.

3. **Spot prime** - It's always good practice to 'spot prime' over plaster fills, joint compound fills, or spackle fills, with a good quality interior latex primer, or interior/exterior acrylic primer before moving on to the paint itself. Tinting the primer to a light gray is often helpful if working with a medium to darker value paint color.

4. **Scuff sand** - Be sure to lightly 'scuff' sand any areas that might still feel a bit rough and remove dust with a vacuum cleaner or dust brush as needed, even after priming, ensuring a dust free surface that will be ready to paint.

5. **Start high** - As a general rule of thumb, most paint job tasks work high to low, not the other way around. That is, work off a short ladder as needed to start at the top of a wall, cutting in along the top of a wall and a ceiling, for example, first. Then, cut in paint along any corners, around light switch cover areas, outlet plug areas, and then along the top of baseboard trim last. Painting with a good quality paint brush, working with an inch worth of paint poured into a *'cut bucket'* (a 5-quart bucket with a handle) works well.

6. **Divide & conquer** - It is always best to have one painter do the 'cut' work first, followed by a second painter doing the 'roll' work immediately after the brush work, if possible.

7. **Double coat** - two coats of paint are standard when painting solid, opaque paint.

8. **Clean up** - Once the paint has had a good opportunity to 'set up' and dry properly, it will be time to carefully remove any painter's tape, restore any previously

removed switch plate covers, fold up the drop cloth, and strike any paints and tools from the space.

A few more thoughts on brushing & rolling

- Use a high quality synthetic bristle paint brush for the cut work, rather than a natural bristle brush, as natural bristle brushes are mostly used for washes or using oil based paints, which are not common in theatrical painting applications.
- Consider using an 18-inch wide roller cover and roller frame set up if you have many large wall surfaces to paint, as it will save time.
- Latex paint additives, such as '*Floetrol*' can be added to your latex and/or acrylic paints to improve the flow and leveling qualities of the paint application and will provide a better finish than simply adding small amounts of water to thicker paint products.
- When rolling paint, first load the paint roller in the tray by rolling down the ramp of the tray several times into the deeper well of the tray that holds the paint. Never start by dunking the roller cover first into the well of the tray.
- First, apply the paint from the roller to the wall surface using an 'N' shape, then 'lay off' the paint in even, uniformly rolled strokes from the top of the wall down to the bottom of the wall. Overlap roller passes as you paint from one side of the wall to the other.

Chapter 5
DRAWING & SCALING 101!

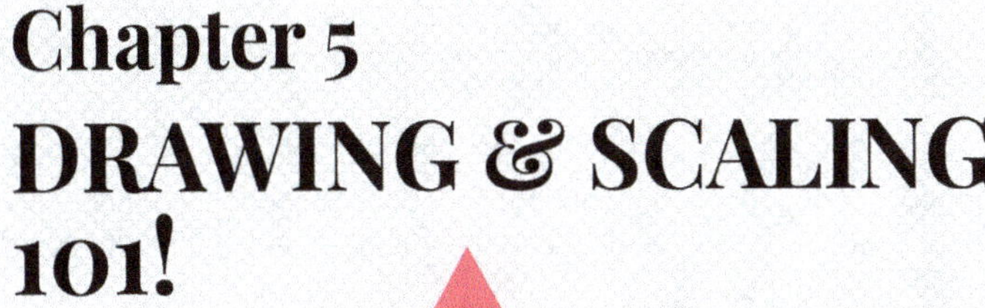

Layout Essentials

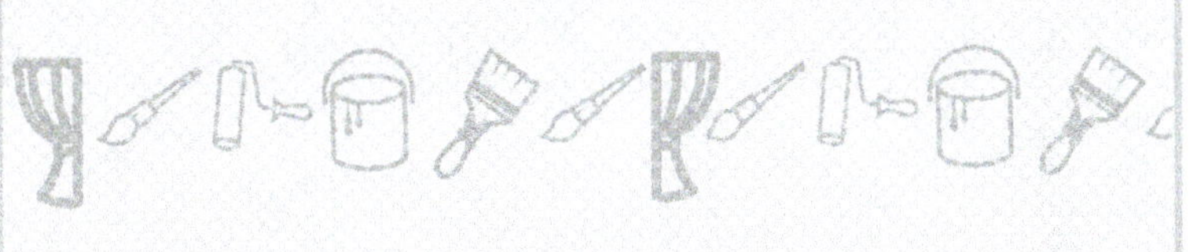

CHAPTER 5
DRAWING & SCALING 101!

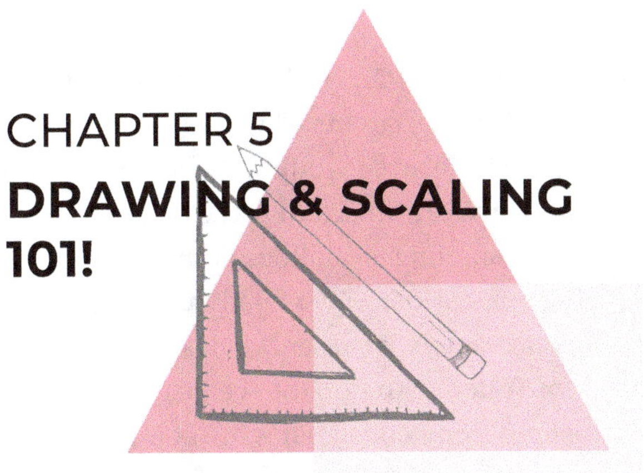

Layout Essentials

NOT EVERYONE WHO PAINTS, or considers themselves a professional painter, or even a scenic artist, believes that they are skilled at drawing. There are some artists and painters who are, more or less, naturally skilled draughtsmen - and for them, the ability to look at a scenic designer's plans & drawings and accurately 'scale up' the design in terms of proportion with particular sensitivity to qualities of line & form, drawing & layout of a design may come fairly easily. For most everyone, however, the ability to accurately scale up, cartoon and clean up a designed drawing to the specs of the design - often larger than life-size or larger - is more a set of learned skills and applied craft, rather than the result of intuitive, artistic talent at work. We will take a look at some tried and true methods for working with scale, proportion and accuracy in reproducing line work in full scale here.

. . .

Measuring , Scaling Up & Drawing Methods

1. **MEASURE TWICE DRAW ONCE** - if the old adage that carpenters use "measure twice, cut once" works for constructing scenery, a scenic artist would follow the "measure twice, draw once" approach to make certain that the proportionality and linear qualities of the 'line-work' they are laying out, cartooning & finally painting on a piece of scenery accurately represents a designer's plan in full scale. More often than not, the scenic painter will take a measurement from a designer's full color, scaled, painted version of their design (known as a *'paint elevation'*) using a *scale ruler* to obtain accurate measurements to work with. Specifically, the scenic painter will use an *architect's scale ruler* - working with the scale noted on the designer's plan/drawing/paint elevation - and follow with the full scale measurement on the piece of scenery, or backdrop, etc, they are working on. As an example, if a scenic designer has noted that their paint elevation has been drawn at a scale of 1/2" (that is, *1/2" = 1'-0" scale*), then the scenic painter will take all necessary measurements from the drawing/paint elevation using the 1/2" scale side of the scale ruler. In 1/2" scale, a line that is drawn to be half an inch long on the designer's drawing/paint elevation will be equal to one foot on the full scale piece of scenery. This concept holds true for any scale in which a designer chooses to draw their plans.

2. **STAY ON THE GRID** - the oldest, and most often relied upon method for 'scaling up' a design is the *grid method*. By drawing, or overlaying, a grid of evenly spaced squares over the designer's drawing/paint elevation, the scenic painter can give themselves an accurate means to reproduce a drawing in full scale. To be more specific, if

the design has been indicated to be 1/2" scale then a grid of half inch by half inch square can be overlayed on the drawing/paint elevation. In turn, a full scale grid that is made from one foot wide by one foot wide squares will be drawn or overlayed on the full scale piece of scenery. Any drawn line or shape that falls inside a particular square, or across a particular coordinate point on the designer's drawing/paint elevation will be reproduced in the corresponding square and/or coordinate point on the scenery. Typically, a scenic painter might use a chalkline (a *'snap-line'*) to apply a temporary grid to the scenery after first applying a coat of primer or white paint. I find it easy, and cleaner, to overlay a continual grid using brightly colored construction string on a backdrop or piece of scenery that is laying flat on a paint shop floor. The string line may be tacked down using a staple gun every foot, or using tape to hold the string grid in place temporarily while the scenic painter sketches/ 'cartoons' the design using vine charcoal, or chalk. Once the drawing has been completed, the string may be removed, excess charcoal can be *'flogged'* off using a hand-made *flogger tool* (a length of pole, or stick, with strips of muslin attached at one end), and the cartooned drawing is then cleaned up and *'inked'* - effectively 'locking' it in place using a permanent marker. Painting comes next.

3. **PROJECT WHAT YOU SEE** - just as many old masters utilized the optical and mechanical devices of their time, devices such as the *camera obscura* or the *camera lucida*, scenic painters will sometimes use a projector to reproduce a design accurately in full scale on a piece of scenery. There is, however, an asterisk of importance that should always be placed next to the notion of using a projector to 'do the work' for the painter; that is, simply using a projector and assuming that everything will end

up being perfect is a common misconception. Let me explain. All projectors, in varying degrees, will distort a projected image. This distorted effect is known as *'keystoning.'* Because the proportional accuracy of a projected image relies on the results of light passing through a lens, it is important to make sure that both the projector and wall, flat or piece of scenery, are truly placed parallel to each other and the projector is not projecting light & image at an angle. This is, effectively, keystoning. It is recommended to position the center of the projector, or the lens of the projector as close to the center of the wall or scenic flat as possible to minimize the effect of proportional distortions. In many newer, digital projectors, keystoning can be adjusted to some degree. Older format projectors, such as overhead projectors and opaque projectors, will reliably produce some optical distortion. It is recommended to project, essentially, individual 'squares' of the full scale image separately; moving the projector accordingly for each square or section that is projected and traced. Typically, I will mark off scenery that is being projected on every 6-8 feet to minimize the effects of key stoning. Some projectors even produce a bright enough light and image that a painter can apply some paint while projecting, rather than always projecting and tracing in a darkened room and painting afterward.

4. **WAITING TO POUNCE** - another reliable method for transferring a drawing from one source to what will become painted scenery is to transfer a full scale line drawing/design by *'pouncing'* it. This age-old technique is a useful method of taking a full scale sketch, or 'cartoon' that has been drawn on paper and accurately transferring it onto another surface, on which the design can then be inked and painted. It is also a great way to repeat a smaller design motif that needs to be repeated

and painted several times (other methods for direct paint application of a repeatable design would include working with a hand cut stencil, or creating a stamp). Basically, after the design has been drawn on paper (or printed on paper), tiny holes are then continuously punched out along the lines of the drawing using a pounce wheel tool. Placing a piece of felt or a piece of insulating foam underneath the drawing that is being traced with the pounce wheel is a helpful way to assist the tool. After the pounce wheel tracing is completed, the pattern is then positioned and temporarily taped or weighted so it may not move when pouncing. A 'pounce bag' (a square of fabric, such as muslin containing pigmented powder, tied up with string or elastic at the top; can be made of several layers of cheesecloth or even an old sock) is then used to release powdered charcoal or powdered chalk by means of occasional tapping and rubbing the bag over the design - thereby transferring the lines of the design to the surface that will be painted, whether it is a hard-covered or a soft-covered surface.

5. **TRANSFERABLE SKILLS** - in keeping with the idea of transferring a full scale drawing on paper to a paintable substrate, another variation on the pouncing/transferring method is to transfer a design via a *rubbing* method. Essentially, it is generally effective to turn the drawing over to the back side of the paper and scribble or rub on some kind of drawing medium, whether it be heavy graphite/lead markings from a pencil or stick charcoal and then re-trace the original design from the front of the paper using a firm hand (a ballpoint pen will often work for this). In this manner, the original design can be transferred to the new surface that will be painted.

6. **PUT IT IN PRINT** - finally, in lieu of hand-drawing, pouncing, projecting or tracing a design in full scale there

is always the option to print a full color version of the designer's artwork/design and apply it to a primed/prepared surface for use on the scenery itself. This method of getting the 'art' on the scenery quickly can certainly be effective, but can have its drawbacks too. If printing a very complex painted design seems like the best way to go, due to time constraints or other considerations, it is best to be sure to think of the following things: fidelity, surface, saturation, smoothness & subtlety. By this, I mean that the accuracy - fidelity - of the print will depend on the quality of the artwork contained in the designer's digital file. The resolution, or format of the image file should be a relatively high resolution image - at least 150 to 300dpi (dots per inch) to not appear pixelated in printed form. The surface, or quality, of the paper that the color print is printed on is always a factor - flat bond paper will produce a duller color print than more expensive, glossier paper stocks or other printable papers. Be sure to run a test print and check the saturation, or richness of the print. Adjustments might need to be made to the printer or to the original, source file. Smoothness directly relates to how the printed paper is adhered to the scenery or flats being used; my advice, if possible, is to use wallpaper paste to adhere prints to the scenery rather than using spray adhesives. Lighter weight papers may need to be sealed first on both sides with a thin coat of clear shellac prior to adhering with wallpaper paste in order to keep the printed paper from buckling in a noticeable way. And, in terms of a final, visually acceptable, 'subtle' aesthetic, it may also be useful to overpaint some or all of the color print with paints, tinted glazes or even pastels or other mediums in order to achieve the desired aesthetic that a production demands.

Chapter 6
MIXOLOGY!

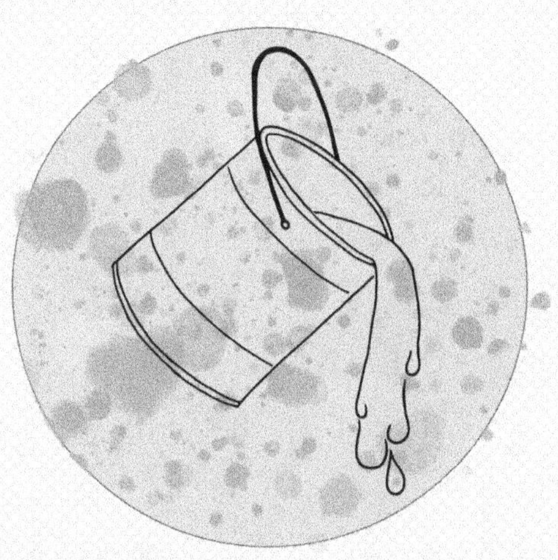

Mixing Paint &
Working With Color

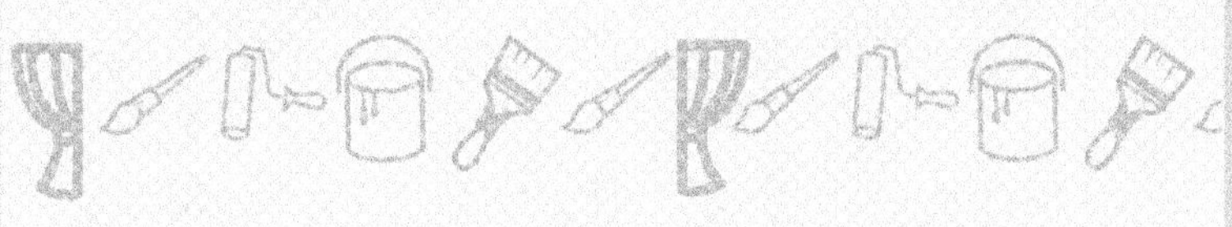

CHAPTER 6
MIXOLOGY!

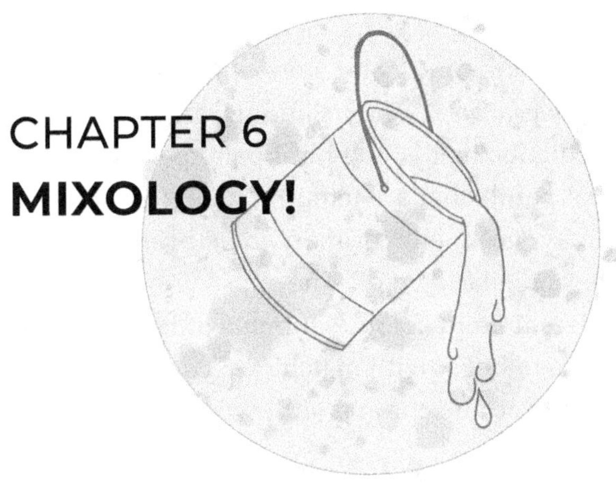

M ixing Paint and Working with Color

WORKING with color and custom mixing paints is often as much of an art as it is a science. Color, basic color theory & color mixing can be at once incredibly simple and frustratingly complex - but it is important to keep in mind that working with color is more of a learned skill than an intuitive skill. We will do the best to cover the basic skills & concepts you may need to know in this chapter.

The basics of color, rather the basics of working with color in the form of additive, opaque pigments, is something most everyone has at least an elementary knowledge of: *primary colors* are red, yellow and blue; *secondary colors* (an equal mix of any two primary colors) are orange, green and purple. From there, things get a bit more complicated.

Tertiary colors - *tertiary colors* can be best described as colors produced by the mixing together of a primary color with a non-complementary secondary color (ie, the hyphenated colors). For example, yellow-green is a mix of a primary color, yellow, and a secondary color, green. Blue-violet is a mix of blue and purple. Red-orange a mix of red and orange, and so on.

In theory, painters can mix any color they will need to work with, as long as they have a basic understanding of color theory and the right raw ingredients; that is, the right paint colors to start from. The most essential paints that are required to mix most every color that a painter may need are: primary red, primary blue, primary yellow, white and black paint. The most useful way to think about mixing different paint colors - in terms of being able to 'match' a certain color - is to begin with matching 3 components, or factors: the hue, the value and the chroma of the color that is being matched.

THE 3 FACTORS TO Match While Mixing Paint Colors:

1. **HUE** - the *Hue* of a color is, effectively, the main raw ingredient required to match a paint color. The hue of a color will be closest to *one* of the primary colors; red, yellow or blue. The hue of a color is typically the starting point.

2. **VALUE** - the *Value* of a color is, essentially, identifying how light or dark a color may be. On a visual scale of 1 to 9, with 1 being white and 9 being black, and 5 being a so called 'medium gray,' any color may be matched to its proper value. This is useful to understand, as any color that falls above a number 5 in terms of value will need to have some white pigment added to it. If a color is as light in value as, say, a number 2 value then it will most likely start from white pigment. Every color has a value associated with it.

3. **CHROMA** - the *Chroma* of a color represents how saturated, pure, or intense the pigment is. Chroma is also

known as the 'key' of a color. A high chroma paint color is typically warm, while a low chroma paint color is typically cool - but not always. If one thinks of different tones of yellow paint pigments, for example, there are high chroma yellows - such as lemon yellow - but also low chroma yellows - such as yellow ochre or raw sienna.

HELPFUL COLOR MIXING Tips (Important Things To Know):

THERE ARE 2 DISTINCT COLOR WHEELS - There are 2 distinct color wheels that a painter will work from; a standard pigment based color wheel *and* a CMYK based color wheel. In working to identify the correct hue of a color when color mixing, it is possible that the closest raw pigment is not closest to a standard primary red, yellow or blue but *may* be closest to a CMYK primary color - cyan, magenta, yellow - as used in printing inks. Cyan is known as a process blue and is, effectively, similar to turquoise blue or sky blue (containing more yellow, and higher chroma than standard primary blue, like pthalo blue or cobalt blue). Magenta is readily identified in its own right as an available pigment and is useful when mixing saturated red violets and purples. The yellow here is closer to a lemon yellow, sometimes known as hansa light yellow and is also generally brighter yellow-green than a standard yellow pigment, such as cadmium yellow. If the 'wrong' hue has been identified and is required for optimal color matching, then it will be difficult to obtain the 'correct' color match.

UNDERSTAND COMPLEMENTARY COLORS - a complementary color is the color that is the opposite or complement of a color on a color wheel. That is, red vs green/yellow vs purple/blue vs orange. By mixing any color with its complement, a painter can easily adjust the intensity of a mixed paint color. Adding complementary colors together with create a neutral color of sorts, in effect a kind of 'gray' in the truest sense of the word (a colorful 'gray' instead of a 'number 5' gray, which is an equal mixture of black and white pigment). As useful examples, a mixed color may be adjusted to be more neutral, or less intense, by adding a complementary color; thereby turning a reddish orange into a warm brown by adding in greenish-blue. A maroon red can be created by adding a green or purple into a yellowish red or into a reddish orange.

TINT AND SHADE - by adding white to any color, a tint will be created, raising the value of a mixed color. Adding black pigment to any color will create a shade, lowering the value of a mixed color.

EARTH TONES - in addition to using the primary colors, along with white and black pigments when mixing colors, painters may also mix or incorporate *'earth tones'* into their mixing and painting arsenal. There are four earth tones: burnt umber, raw umber, burnt sienna and raw sienna. Essentially, burnt umber is a sort of warm chocolate brown, raw umber is a greenish/muddy brown, burnt sienna is a brick-like red clay brown, and raw sienna is a kind of cool mustard yellow/brown.

AVOID ADDING BLACK IF POSSIBLE - as a general rule of thumb when color mixing, it is useful to adjust both the chroma and the value of the pigment that is being mixed by simply working with red, yellow, blue and white pigments as much as possible - getting as close of a color match as one can while avoiding the use of adding black pigment. Keep in mind that black pigment will tend to dull out a color, often creating a less visually interesting tone than by working with other mixed colors and using complementary colors to deepen a pigment. Black paint, such as a flat 'carbon' black has a visible absence in a painting - in other words, black pigment will absorb light and create, in effect, a visual negative space in a painting; while using a very dark value color, like a blue-black, a green black, a purple-black, etc, will be *'almost-black'* but will still have a visual presence rather than having a visual absence in a painting. Try mixing equal amounts of the 3 primary colors together to create a mixed black first when mixing colors and see what that can do for your color first. Then add in small amounts of black pigment only as needed.

MIX YOUR GRAYS - instead of relying on a mixture of black and white pigment to create a 'gray' paint - which will create a 'cold' *'Number 5'* gray - try to mix more visually interesting 'grays' by working with complementary color pigments, such as yellow and purple and adding white first. These mixed grays will create warmer or more visually interesting tones of 'gray.'

PAINT DRIES DOWN - keep in mind that all water-based acrylics and latex-based paint colors will dry a bit darker than the color might first appear when mixing it. This is referred to as the paint color drying *'down.'* To be sure that you have achieved as close a paint color 'match' as is possible when color mixing, brush a thin swatch of your mixed paint color on a small piece of white paper or index card so it extends all the way to one edge of the paper and dry it with a hair dryer. This small paint swatch, a 'draw-down' card, will represent the exact mixed color, including the value of the color and can be compared with the paint elevation or other sample that you might be working from.

COLOR IS PERCEPTUAL - how we *see* color, rather how we *perceive* color is relative. As such, color is affected by many factors: the trueness or temperature of the light one is viewing the color in, which color or colors are being viewed next to the painted pigment color, and how one individually 'sees' or *receives* color. Josef Albers, the modern artist, color theorist and teacher, who is primarily known for his *Homage To The Square* series (abstract paintings, based on his long study of the principles and effects of color theory) wrote *Interaction of Color*, 1963. *Interaction of Color* reinforces his notion that color 'is almost never seen as it really is" since it is subject to being perceptually altered or affected by the singular conditions it is experienced in at the present moment. Color perception must always be considered by the painter when mixing, exploring and applying paint colors.

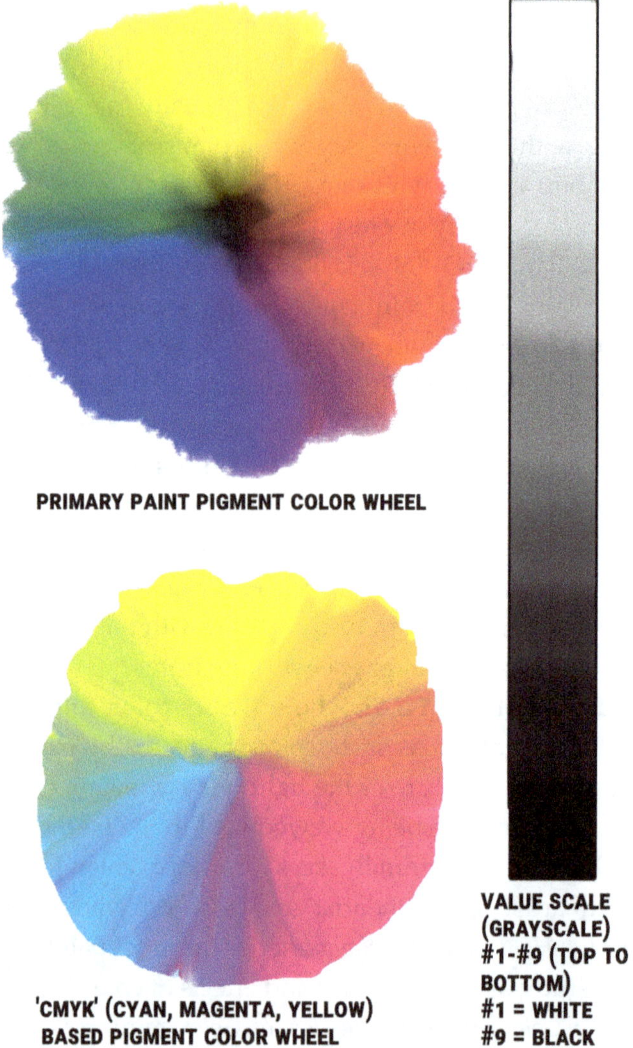

PRIMARY PAINT PIGMENT COLOR WHEEL

'CMYK' (CYAN, MAGENTA, YELLOW) BASED PIGMENT COLOR WHEEL

VALUE SCALE (GRAYSCALE) #1-#9 (TOP TO BOTTOM) #1 = WHITE #9 = BLACK

. . .

FOR A FEW ADDITIONAL useful paint color and mixing tips, also refer to one of the upcoming chapters (*Chapter 9 - 'Age Old Aging!'*) which includes a couple of key paint color mixing approaches that will help your scenic painting.

Chapter 7
BETTER WITH TEXTURE!

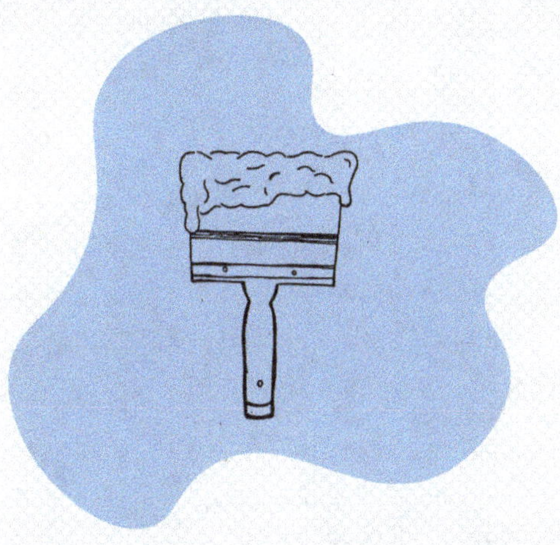

Texture Coating Application

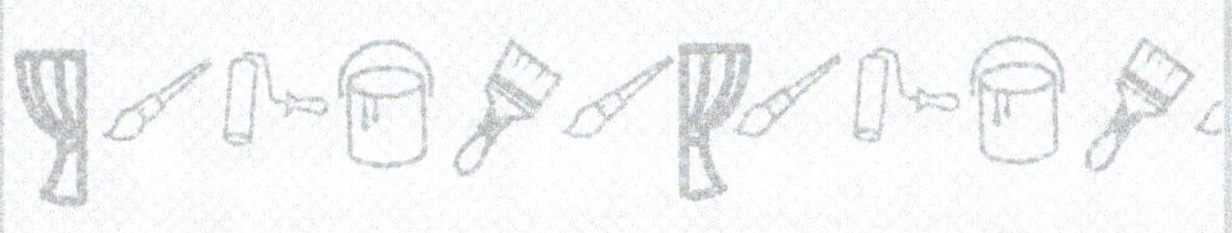

CHAPTER 7
BETTER WITH TEXTURE!

Texture Coating Application

SOME OF THE most effective scenic painting techniques seen on stage, under final stage-lighting, incorporate not only color but also the application of various scenic texture coatings. Any scenic painter's 'tool kit' of knowledge is enhanced by a solid working knowledge of different texturing materials that are available, along with an understanding of different application methods for achieving effective texture coatings on painted scenery. In this chapter, I provide an overview of some tried-and-true tools, materials and application methods that will bring more depth - actual depth - in the form of texture to your painted scenery.

Assorted Texturing Materials:

The list of handy and often essential materials that a theatrical paint shop will have in stock to achieve various custom mixtures to be used for creating texture coatings effects on painted scenery include the following list. Brief descriptions of each materials and their possible uses are also included below.

1. **Joint compound** - sold as traditional 'heavy' or light weight ready-mixed batches, joint compound - also called *drywall compound* or *'mud'*- is a must have item in any paint shop. Can be used straight from the container as a good utility filling material for staple and screw-holes, it is also effective as a 'skim-coat' (an even, thin, troweled application) over the entire surface of a hard covered flat to minimize the look of wood grain; good for hiding seams along with drywall paper tape or fiberglass mesh tape. Drawback is that it has a somewhat slow dry-time and may require some sanding to produce a very smooth surface finish, however it is a cost-effective, must have item. Incorporated into custom scenic 'dope' / 'roping' mixes (see later in this chapter, *custom texture coating mixes*).

2. **Sand** - bags of sand, usually found in masonry supply areas of hardware supply stores, can create an effective texture (faux stucco looks) when added directly into paints or 'broadcast' (spread evenly across the surface) into freshly applied paints, sealers and other coatings. May be used to provide a 'non-skid' finish on painted steps as needed. Look for 'play-sand' in the supply stores.

3. **Glue** - various types of water-soluble glues (resins) are very useful in scenic painting applications. PVA (polyvinyl acetate) - ie, white glue - is the most

commonly used glue in most paint shops, however wood glue also has its applications (notably, used underneath a paint coating to create the look of cracks or aging), and more specialized theatrical flex glue is also used widely on theatrical scenery, primarily to coat sculpted foam, but other options are effective and more widely available.

4. **Sawdust** - another commonly found shop material, sawdust can be added to paint and glue to make a convincing faux rust texture on painted steel-look sets, as well as being mixed into compounds. Also highly useful in paint shops for absorbing leftover water-based paints for safe disposal.

5. **Plaster** - plaster is another broad category, contained many types of useful, dry-powder based texturing and filling materials. Some of the most useful as used on painted scenery include *Plaster of Paris* (which is a fast-setting, smooth plaster useful in quick patching applications as well as in coating sculpted foams and in small casting); *base coat plaster* - otherwise known as 'brown-coat' or 'scratch-coat' plasters - can create very effective and relatively lightweight textures that simulate concrete, bricks & mortar, and organic rock and tree bark textures as well (use with a bonding adhesive glue, and seal with a clear finish or a thinned water-based acrylic-latex primer before painting); *setting-type joint compound powder* is extremely useful and is, technically, a gypsum plaster - and is great for filling holes, seams and deeper imperfections on scenery without shrinking or cracking that may result from using joint compound only for 'deep' holes.

6. **Elastomeric** - a type of thick, polymer coating, elastomeric paints create a waterproof coat on wood and other surfaces. Elastomeric acrylic (roof coating) is an effective, thick, brushable white primer that may be applied to hard covered wood flats, often helping to

eliminate the look of fine wood grain. When mixed with joint compound, elastomeric acrylic creates a versatile, 'all-purpose' shop texture coat material that may be applied to scenic units, including floors, walls, steps and platforms. Adheres well to many foams and fabrics.

7. **Thickeners** - many materials may be used in conjunction with paints as paint 'thickeners.' Some useful products that may be added to paints include: clear hair gels, white glue, wallpaper paste.

8. **Caulk** - otherwise known as 'painter's caulk,' water-based latex and acrylic-latex caulk has many great applications for a paint shop that works on painted theatrical scenery. The most common application for painter's caulk is, of course, evenly filling small gaps along the edges of applied trim moldings, but may also be used for fast filling of small seams and staple holes (20-minute dry caulk recommended here), and bonding small pieces of applied details, adhesive for quick fabric/muslin 'dutchman' patches, and for relatively small areas to be painted as combed-texture 'wood' looks.

9. **Wood filler** - wood filler products, specifically water-soluble or water-cleanup wood filler products, are handy to have in a paint shop. 'Ready-mixed' latex wood fillers make quick work for the occasional patching of holes since they may be painted generally very quickly; powdered wood filler products, like 'Durham's' and others have a variety of applications when used alone, for filling or even small casting as well as mixed with water based glue.

Assorted Texturing Tools:

- **Putty knife/knives** - typically 1, 4, and 6 inch wide drywall mud 'putty' knives are the most commonly used 'texturing' tools for painters. Used mostly for small filling and coating applications; also for scraping and cleaning dried paint from buckets

- **Taping knifes/ Drywall taping knives** - larger, flat-edged 'taping' knives (usually 8, 10, 12 inch wide) can be used for joint compound skim-coating applications, plaster applications, 'bed-coating' drywall tape on wall seams, paint edging, and for trimming wallpapers with a sharp knife or blade.

- **Pool trowels** - round edged 'pool' or masonry trowels are great for many applied wall textures, including concrete, stucco and plaster looks on scenery - since they will not create sharp 'edge' marks due to the fact that they have no sharp corners.

- **Loop rollers** - standard, 9-inch wide 'loop' rollers, featuring small plastic nubs or 'loops' across the outer surface of the roller cover, are useful to create low decorative textured finishes.

- **Sea sponge rollers** - standard, 9-inch wide roller covers wrapped in organic sea sponge are very useful in creating broadly random 'organic' textures, paint treatments and glaze treatments for painted scenery.

- **Brooms & squeegees** - many different types of standard 'corn' brooms, flat brooms, and prepared/custom cut rubber squeegees can create interesting textured finishes and looks toward a variety of looks; everything from decorative 'fish' scale treatments, to textured strié paint glazes, wood graining and striping.

- **Hopper guns** - a pneumatic (compressed air driven) hopper gun is a large, hand held sprayer that is used to force mixed and thinned texture compounds directly onto a surface. It can produce heavy, medium-sized and finer splatters of texture coating materials. Hopper guns, while a bit heavy and unwieldy - since the weight of the material is held in a triangular molded plastic 'hopper' tank that is located directly above the sprayer - can be useful for applying controlled textures on a large surface or coating unusual, carved, surfaces such as foam 'rocks.' Proper masking of shop walls and floors is needed when working with a hopper gun.

Useful Theatrical Texture Mixes:

BELOW IS a short list of generally useful texture coating mixtures for use on painted theatrical scenery:

1. **Elasto/JC mix** = a 1:1 ratio mixture of elastomeric white acrylic roof coating: ready-mixed joint compound. An almost 'universal' shop texture coating for heavy brush daubing, thick 'slumped' brush coating of theatrical trim moldings, carved foam, faux plaster walls, and many uses.

2. **Scenic 'Dope'/'Roping' Coating** = a mixture of Joint Compound, paint and white glue that can be adjusted both in terms of tinting toward a base paint color and in terms of thickness/thinness by altering the ratio of compound to paint used. White glue adds additional toughness to the dried coating. Effective in both heavy brushed applications as well as roller applications using a very thick nap roller cover. Application of thinned glazes or washes over a scenic dope coating works wonderfully on stage. General mixing ratio of 3:1:5% (that is, approximately 3-4 parts of ready mixed joint compound mixed with 1 part paint with an additional 5% of white glue (PVA) added - often the rough equivalent of covering the entire top surface of the mixture with white glue before mixing thoroughly). Small amounts of powdered joint compound or plaster

may also be added to increase the thickness and/or speed up the cure time of the coating.

3. **Base Coat Plaster 'Cement' Texture Coating** = best for use when replicating realistic/believable concrete, plaster, mortar & brick surfaces, as well as for use on rough, dimensional or slightly sculpted organic shapes such as faux tree branches and rock surfaces. Starting with a commercially available base coat plaster bag mix (such as USG Structo-Lite, and others); often called scratch coat or brown coat plaster. Begin by applying a concrete bonding primer or plaster adhesive to the surface that will be coated. Allow to dry for recommended time before mixing and applying/shaping the base coat plaster mixture. It is recommended to start the mixture process of the base coat plaster in a 5 gallon bucket using an electric drill mixer/mixing blade. Add some water first into the bucket before the dry mix is added. Continue to add the recommended amount of water until the proper mixed consistency has been reached (typically a thick but somewhat creamy consistency that 'sticks' to a trowel or large wooden stir stick when held upside-down and does not run or fall off). Use a small amount of bonding primer adhesive or plaster adhesive as an 'add-mix' of glue to the mixed plaster texture. Once the texture has thoroughly dried, overnight, it may be sealed using a thinned water based clear coat, acrylic floor coating/polish or sealer, or 'primed' with a water based acrylic latex primer diluted with water. After that, the texture may be painted or glazed as desired; an additional layer of scenic dope coating may also be added to provide toughness and more 'smoothness' to the more rough base coat plaster texture if desired.

Chapter 8
THINK THIN!

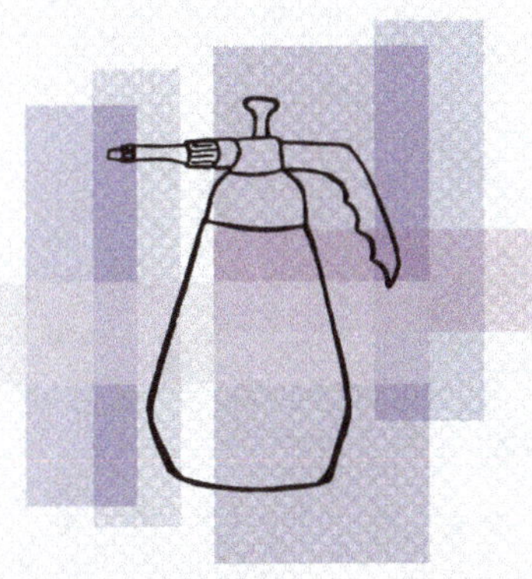

Working With
Washes, Glazes & Sprays

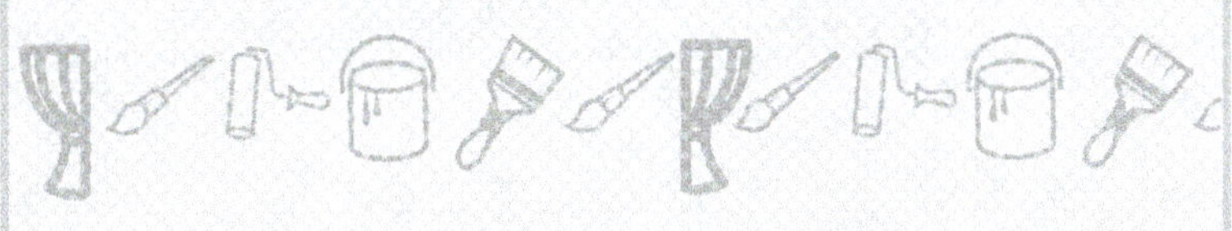

CHAPTER 8
THINK THIN!

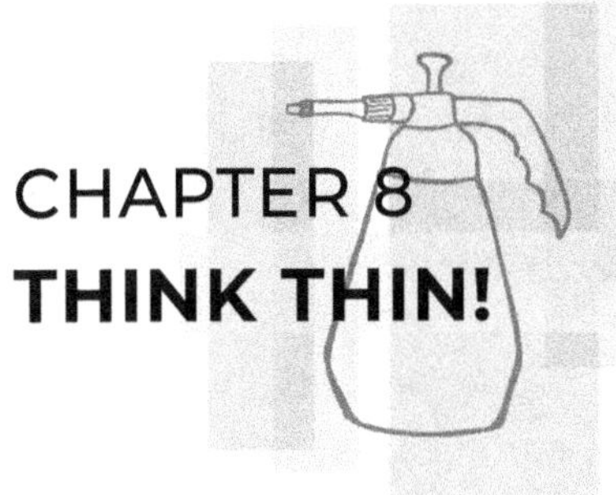

Working with Washes, Sprays and Glazes

While most of the 'foundational' scenic painting techniques - the most often utilized basic methods for paint application on painted scenery - rely on the '*wet-blending' (*see: following definitions) and 'scumbling' of creamy, opaque paints that vary in value and tone, it is often thinned paint applications that provide painted depth and brilliance to painted scenery. In every way, working with thinned paints in the form of watercolor 'washes' and learning to control medium-to-fine spray applications and the layering of glazes, brings the best aspects of efficiency, economy & elegance to painted scenery. In this chapter, I will summarize the most useful mixtures, tools and approaches for working with these thinned applications of color, translucent glazes and sprays.

What Are Washes, Glazes & Sprays?:

A few key definitions to help distinguish between the more technical aspects of *washes*, *glazes* and *sprays* for use by the scenic painter are needed to mix and apply them successfully.

1. **Washes** - the term '*wash*' and '*watercolor*' essentially mean the same thing for use in scenic painting applications. A watercolor 'wash' can be defined as a painting medium that is created by mixing a pigment, or concentrated color, with water; so that the ratio of pigment:water is at least 1:20 (or more). Watercolor paint washes allow for broad, quick, soft applications of vibrant color layers in a subtractive painting process; that is, the translucent layer of watercolor wash allows the white of the painted ground to show through. Instead of mixing white pigment to create lighter values in the painting, the white background (or other color background) is allowed to be partially or completely visible. Often, when painting 'watercolor' passages on backdrops and other scenery, it is typical for a thin 'film' or layer of water to be applied first, followed by the thinned paint/color wash; allowing for a soft painted look on a relatively large scale to be achieved.

2. **Glazes** - a '*glaze*' is a painting medium created by adding pigment to a clear binder (clear-coat). Typically, glazes are mixed by using concentrated theatrical scenic paint, diluted artist grade acrylic paint, or universal tint and stirring small amounts of a color into a water-based clear binder, such as a clear flat vinyl-acrylic, or a clear satin to clear gloss acrylic polyurethane. Colorful glazes mixed with glossier sealers can effectively emulate the look of stained glass, for example, and earth tones mixed with clear flat binders and water make useful shadowing and

aging glazes. The base-painted color and/or scenic painting underneath the translucent layer(s) of glaze will show through.

3. **Sprays** - theatrical scenic painters often use medium-sized ('garden' or 'floretta' sprayers) to large-sized ('Hudson') tank sprayers filled with strained mixtures of washes and loosened glazes to spray layers of color in the form of fine spray gradients to medium dot-pattern spatters on painted floors, backdrops and scenic flats. Commercially available strainer bags or layers of fine cheesecloth combined with a funnel is recommended for filling spray mixes into tank sprayers. Spray application of flame-treating liquid 'saturant' solutions is also common.

4. **Spatters** - the term *'spatter'* or *'spatters'* when applied to scenic painting techniques usually refers to a painter dipping a wide, flat brush into a loosened paint glaze or wash and creating broad, organically sized 'dots' of paint on a surface that is being painted on a shop floor. The brush may be tapped on the palm of the hand or a stick to create a spatter effect. Spatters are commonly used to create the look and appearance of granite, rock and other organic surfaces.

5. **Organic glazes** - the term *'organic glaze'* refers to a unique and effective layered wet-on-wet glazing technique that can create varied and visually interesting looks on painted scenery. Essentially, this technique starts first with a loosely and broadly hand-spattered layer/partial layer of water (or water with a small amount of Murphy's oil soap added into it), followed immediately by a spatter of tinted glaze color, followed immediately again by another spatter of slightly soapy water - or isopropyl alcohol, denatured alcohol, or other liquid. As the water and other 'reactive' liquid gradually air dries, a uniquely varied and 'broken' glaze treatment is left

behind. This technique can be very effective in creating faux marble, stone, concrete and other surface effects. Try broadcasting the water/liquid/glaze/alcohol, etc *up* into the air rather than *down* on to the painted scenery like a traditional spatter technique.

6. **Gradients/Ombré sprays** - the subtle shifting from one color to another color, or from dark to light values shifting across a painted floor or other painted scenic unit when evenly applying sprayed paints is known as a *'gradient'* or an *'ombré'* treatment. One very common application of a small scale gradient is the traditional painting of thinned paint or glaze to create the look of naturally occurring shadows on painted scenery by first applying one pass, or 'line' of shadow paint medium/mix followed immediately by a slightly overlapping painted pass of water or clear finish on a second brush, which creates a soft outer edge, or gradient. This is typically created by using two scenic fitch brushes, one for the shadow color and one for the 'clear' medium or water.

7. ***Wet-blending** - wet-blending is a term that describes one of the foundational/fundamental scenic painting techniques (along with scumbling, spattering, sponging, 'X-pattern'/cross-pattern base coating & dragging/combing). The term 'wet-blending' is a scenic painting technique in which two paint colors are applied next to each other and softly blended together, creating a transition color in between. Considered 'wet' blending not because the paints are truly loose wash mixes, but the distinct colors must remain wet in order to create an effectively painted blend.

Chapter 9
AGE-OLD 'AGING' !

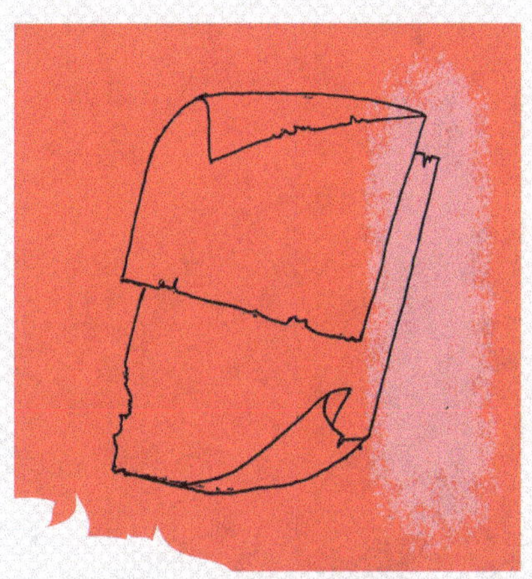

Techniques For Making New Scenery Look, Well, Not-So-New

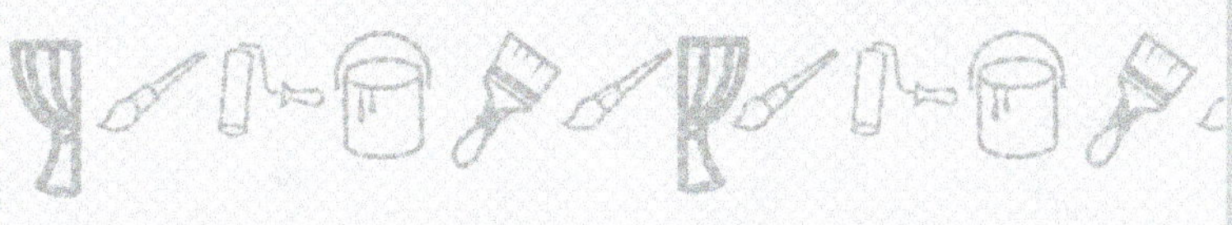

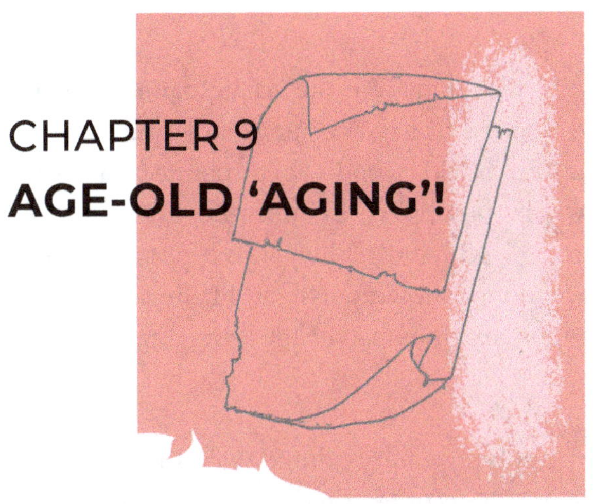

CHAPTER 9
AGE-OLD 'AGING'!

Techniques for Making New Scenery Look, Well, Not-So-New

EMULATING the look and feel of the 'real world' in the painting of theatrical scenery often relies not just on the accurate representation of textures and colors, but also on the subtle to dramatic visual effects of weathering and 'aging.' The scenic painter often uses the term 'aging' when referring to the process of applying paints, washes, glazes and other materials to painted scenery in a wide variety of ways. In this chapter, I will provide some useful information about common, and not as common, paint materials and approaches for making newly built and painted scenery look, well, not-so-new.

AGING TECHNIQUES:

THE LIST of unique aging techniques for the scenic painter is truly varied and is generally derived from a specific weathering or aging effect as seen on plaster, brick, wood, aged painted surfaces, signage, glass windows, metal objects, interior and exterior walls and many other sources. I will most likely leave out a favorite painted aging technique in the following list, but I believe that each of the techniques provided are quite useful for achieving a specific look.

1. **Age-washes** - by applying a very diluted wash of pigment on a painted and/or textured piece of painted scenery using a wide, soft-bristle brush on an extension pole or by spray application using a floretta or Hudson-type tank sprayer, scenery is commonly aged using an 'age-wash' and will make it look not-so-new ('taking the edge off' of the scenery, as a painter might say). A good tip is to first apply a sprayed 'film' of water with a healthy amount of Murphy's Oil Soap added in just before spraying/applying the age wash itself. The addition of the oil soap into the water will soften or 'break' the edges, the surface tension of the paint and water as natural drying occurs, leaving a softer look than by simply using water and paint only.

2. **Grunge-aging** - *'grunge'* aging is the term used for adding the look of dirt or grunge to painted scenery. Mostly, this will be seen as a kind of visual 'halo' of darker paint material in corners and interior edges of dimensional paneling, and along the bottom edges of walls. Paste wax tinted with a raw umber universal tint, used as a medium to grunge-age shiny hardware, including doorknobs and other handled items, can be

effective. Clear flat finishes may also be tinted with universal tint (including raw umber) or paint pigments, such as raw umber or a black/brown mix made of black and burnt umber paint. Van Dyke brown is a useful aging color as well.

3. **Rain-aging** - replicating the subtle effects of weathering, rain and general exposure to the elements on painted scenery, specifically on painted signage. Often achieved by an initial full spray of water and/or water with some soap added, followed immediately by a spray of thinned aging wash that has a slight raw umber color as well as some warm white/gray added. Use a thick nap roller to soften (*'backroll'*), lightly working it in an upward direction across the drying wash. The aim of the rain-aging mixture is typically to achieve slight aging effects on both the lighter and darker areas that have been painted on the sign. Recommended using flat latex paint for this process, due to the way it naturally, finely 'breaks apart' when applied in the manner described.

4. **Block-aging** - *'block-aging'* is a simple, yet effective technique that creates the appearance of chipped paint - mostly along the edges of furniture items, painted walls and scenery. Block-aging paints are applied using two small, hand-held flat wooden blocks (one used as a small palette, the second to apply aging paint), and paint is applied in a low 'shearing,' tapping or skimming motion. Two colors block-aged together work very well. Paint may be thickened if needed with plaster, wallpaper paste and combinations of both to produce larger, more visually convincing 'chipped paint' aging effects.

5. **Character aging** - the term *'character aging'* refers to any scenic-painted effect that appears to be the result of any human (character) interaction that naturally occurs to items that would be touched, walked upon, or otherwise

handled. This can include the look of 'dirty' handprints and handling around cabinet door hardware and doorknobs, as well as scuffs and scrape marks, walking path 'wear' marks, and even more physical 'wear and tear' damage (ie, 'distressing').

6. **Distressing** - physical 'wear and tear' damage effects, artificially created by a scenic painter, or carpenter would count as '*distressing*.' A variety of methods can be employed to create different types of physical distressing aging marks including, but not limited to: sanding, Sur-forming or rasping sharp wooden edges, grinding, hammering, beating scenery with custom distressing tool(s) often made by attaching short lengths of chain, bolts and washers to wooden handle(s) and distortion by bending items.

7. **Resist-aging** - any combination that pairs two separate mediums in a scenic painting process with the intent of utilizing one medium to effectively mask off some part of the scenery while using the other product to paint or age it and/or produce a novel paint effect. In essence, the idea of maintaining a certain amount of previously painted 'negative' space for any resist-aging method can be a creative, effective scenic painting approach. Some resist method techniques include: *chemical resist* (mixing opposing or slightly reactive, generally water-soluble chemicals with thinned water-based paints, washes and glazes; as in spattering of denatured alcohol, glass cleaning solutions, etc., to achieve organic 'marble' - like looks), *masking resist* (applying a semi-solid resist material such as kitty litter, sand, saw dust, wallpaper paste, joint compound, mud, peat moss, wax, liquid latex, etc., to mask a painted surface while applying additional colors). The masking resist is removed after the applied paint has dried, and *organic shield/mask resist* (use of any torn material such as cardboard, paper or

loose fabric as masking device for spray applications to achieve an organic, non-regular edged look).

8. **Alternate/unconventional aging techniques** - many alternate, non-traditional materials and products may be experimented with to create the look of aging effects on painted scenery. Many different types of 'food' or 'beverage' related products can be effective materials to work with, including tea-staining (for fabric), coffee and coffee-ground aging (coffee may have some clear binder and small amounts of raw umber pigment added for use as effective, natural looking aging, while adding ground coffee to glue and paint creates great rust looks), soap (applied to glass and allowed to dry, in the form of natural vegetable oil soap along with some pigment or tint and water for effective wall aging), adding in dry goods such as steel cut oats or corn flakes for use on faux 'peeling' or 'flaking' finishes; also may include the simultaneous use of water sprayed against a spray paint color for believable oxidation, weathering and rusted looks - assuming proper ventilation, of course; and the use of novelty 'silly string' spray as a temporary marble veining mask (string-like foam spray adhesive can also be used for this purpose, but may require additional removal later in the process using a paint thinner).

9. **Rolling and brushing alternates** - often, the most effective ways to achieve quick layers of depth, aging effects and to show off textures involve the use of brushes or rollers/roller covers to add a scenic look. Some of the most notable might include: *dry-brushing* (that is, working a disposable, flat brush - such as a chip brush on a flat piece of cardboard with a small amount of paint, until the paint is whisked 'dry' and quickly applied over a painted surface or a texture), *wet dry-brushing* (an interesting spin on traditional dry-brush technique that adds a mist of water to the surface that is

to be dry-brushes prior to the brushing application), 'hard roller' (use of a smooth rubber covered 'hard' roller to apply a paint or a glaze directly over previously textured and painted surfaces or in combination with a second hard roller and paint material to add variation and, typically, add subtle highlighting).

Chapter 10
TO SEAL & PROTECT!

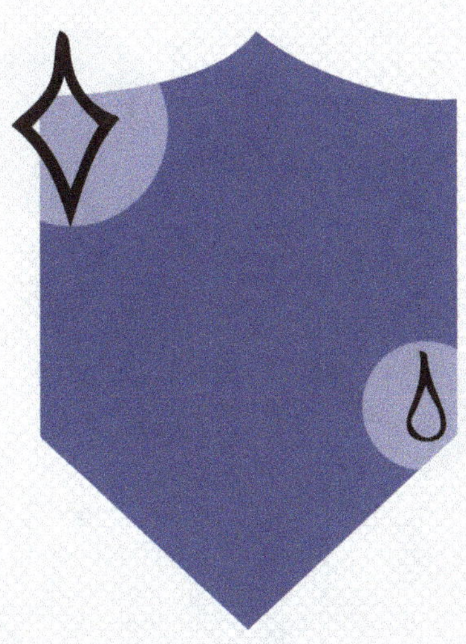

Clear Coat Finishes

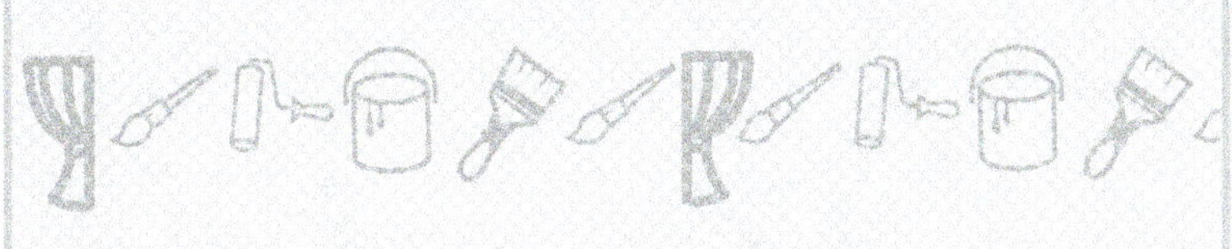

CHAPTER 10
TO SEAL & PROTECT!

Clear Coat Finishes

ONE FINAL, important technical consideration for completing and finishing your painted scenery is figuring out the best way to seal & protect it. This can be achieved by a final application of a variety of clear (*'clear coat'*) sealers - and these clear coatings may be applied in different ways, depending on the visual goals and the production demands of the scenery.

As with deciding which particular combination of paints, colors, painting tools and methods of application, selecting the 'right' clear coat finishing products is based on two things: the designer's aesthetic concerns (in this case, whether or not a piece of painted scenery should appear as a flat, matte, satin, semi-gloss or glossy finish) and the functional production demands that the painted scenery is required to provide (essentially, is the painted and clear-coated scenery functioning as mainly visual or decorative or does is require lots of handling or need to act as a painted surface to walk or to dance on). These two factors, the artistic 'form' and the practical 'function' that the painted scenery should provide always inform the painter which product(s) and application methods will be best in each case.

Benefits & Uses of Clear Coatings:

The following list provides some the key benefits and results of using clear coatings and sealers on painted scenery.

1. **Added durability/wearability** - clear finishes most notably add extra toughness and durability to painted sets. Often, scenery is painted using multiple thin, subtle layers of washes. By applying clear sealer on top of the somewhat 'delicate' scenic painting, the painter ensures that the scenery will be able to withstand moving and performance requirements.

2. **More water resistance** - particularly for use on painted stage platforms, stairs, decking and flooring - but also on painted countertops and other surfaces, clear coats provide the ability for stage crews to mop and clean painted surfaces to maintain show-ready scenery. On some productions, there is even a 'special effects' requirement of fake blood on painted scenery and even rain or water on stage. In these cases, employing the most waterproof clear sealers becomes quite important (ie, using urethane and epoxy based clear coatings).

3. **Deepens color** - adding a layer of clear sealer will make painted colors appear deeper, richer, more saturated. This is particularly true for higher sheens, such as semi-gloss and gloss clear.

4. **Options for different sheens** - for different areas of painted scenic units on stage, there are often visual and performance benefits for varying the sheen(s) of the

painted scenery (ie, clear flat, matte and satin on wall surfaces like painted plaster or faux concrete and 'old' wood; satin sheens or semi-gloss sheens on painted/faux stone, marble, and finished furniture or decorative panelling; gloss clear finishes on high wear dance floor areas, etc). Having 'aging' glazes for use in creating areas of 'dirt' in corners, etc, a flat sheen looks great sitting next to a higher sheen of paint treatment.

Different Clear Coating Options & Uses:

THE LIST I have included below summarizes a few of the most utilized 'types' of clear coat finishing products for use on painted scenery as well as some suggested uses/ areas of application.

1. **Clear vinyl acrylic** - for traditional painted theater backdrops, wall flats and other scenery, use of specialty (*Rosco, Artist's Choice, Mann Brothers,* etc) clear vinyl acrylic - most often 'flat' clear coat, which requires thinning with water by 50% and more for most applications (spray applied most often).

2. **Clear acrylic (artist's grade matte clear)** - artist's grade (100% acrylic binder) clear coatings are useful for thicker, sometimes more 'controlled' applications when used to create glazes that need to maintain specific graining, combing & ragging effects as they 'hold' their shape/form for drying. May be used to create the look of frosted glass (plexiglas).

3. **Clear acrylic polyurethane** - commercially available clear acrylic polyurethane is a great option for adding a protective, higher sheen to faux finished surfaces, such as decorative marble or cabinetry 'wood' as well as decks and floors. Recommended to use almost full-strength, adding in a small amount (5-10%) of water to ease

application by reducing possible streaking. May be applied (2-3 coats recommended) using a smooth, low-nap roller or applicator pad made for waterborne clear coats , and/or a soft, wide brush (4 to 6 inch width). Adds toughness and durability. Adheres well to plexiglas for creating faux stained glass; tintable with acrylic paints & tints.

4. **Clear oil modified (water cleanup) polyurethane -** among the toughest wearing and most water-resistant of clear coat 'urethane' finishes. This is a hybrid coating, which is a true oil-based clear polyurethane but modified so it has low odor and low voc but cleans up using warm water and soap. Highly recommended on higher sheen finish painted show decks.

5. **Clear acrylic floor polishes (floor coatings made for maintenance/custodial applications)** - typically, high gloss, water-thin clear sealers and polishes that are made and sold specifically for custodial and maintenance use. These commercially available clear polishes are made for use in commercial or mild industrial areas, such as vinyl composite tile hallway flooring. They are fast drying, fast recoat and walking times (30 minutes), cost-effective and may be sprayed, mopped and brushed. High degree of wearability/durability and great when used in painting processes as a 'mid-coat' sealer for faux finishing wood, stone, marble, etc.

6. **Clear shellac/ amber shellac** - more of an 'old-school' or 'traditional' clear coat, clear and amber shellac is not water soluble (it thins and cleans up with denatured alcohol). Shellac clear is highly effective when used as a fast setting clear finish on painted decorative marble and for mixing 'FEV' colors (dye and shellac, mixed with alcohol) for use in faux/theatrical stained glass. Highly recommended for use sealing stock or 'bond' flat printed papers, so that they may be rendered more water-

resistant - allowing for easy application on flat scenery using wallpaper paste. Amber shellac produces a great warm tone over painted faux wood surfaces and is useful for creating a 'tobacco-stained' appearance over painted work. Drawbacks are: high degree of chemical/alcohol type fumes while using - proper ventilation becomes important when working with shellac; shellac can be effected (can turn white or blush) by exposure to water.

..And Finally, <u>Don't</u> forget to flame-treat your finished, painted scenery!

THE HEADING ABOVE SAYS it all. While you are in the process of painting your scenery for *any* performance scenario, it is important to remember that your scenery will require *some* type of flame-treatment before it is truly considered complete, and is ready to be used on stage. Flame-treating is the ultimate form of protection on your finished, painted scenery.

Essentially, there are two different types of flame-treating products typically used for treating painted scenery and scenic units:

1. **Additives** - Flame treating *'additive'* products are typically concentrated liquid solutions that are designed to be added to mixed paint colors as a way to add flame resistant properties to painted scenery. Most of these products are sold in smaller, pre-measured bottles and may be added to mixed gallons of water-based paints (mixing ratio per manufacturer's instructions; as in 'add one 8 ounce bottle of flame treating additive to 1 gallon of water-based acrylic latex paint' for example).

2. **Saturants** - Flame treating liquid *'saturants'* are, as the name implies, water-thin clear liquid solutions that are manufactured to be brushed, rolled, or fully sprayed on any raw scenery; including raw wood framing, plywood, muslin, etc. Generally speaking, a full brush or roller-applied coating will ensure full coverage of the flame-treating saturant liquid. If applying by spray, it is recom-

mended to apply 2 full coverage, sprayed coats.

Note: The primary goal and purpose of this guidebook, ***Practical Painted Scenery: A Guidebook*** is to provide the set painter/scenic painter - whether a new student of scenic painting artistry or a more experienced Journeyman painter - with a concise, yet effectively complete reference that may be used toward theatrical painting. I truly hope that I have achieved some of this goal and have provided a few useful tips along the way.

Since I have written another larger, more comprehensive volume on the topic of scenic painting, ***Scenic Compendium: Techniques, Tools & Tricks for Theatrical Scenic Painting (with Emily Curtis).*** *Publication 2023; JK3 Publishing LLC.* ,I would recommend looking to the *Scenic Compendium* to view a wide range of photographs and illustrations that show examples of the scenic painting techniques and tools that are listed in this *Guidebook* and much more.

As an **addendum** of sorts, before I close this Guidebook, I am including a list of additional techniques that I believe hold enough importance to tack on to this volume, as a way of giving the painter a quick listing of painting options you may want to explore or consider further..

- **Venetian and faux venetian plasters** - troweled applications of tinted plaster to achieve beautifully layered wall treatments with subtle variations and visual 'movement.' Look may also be replicated by troweled applications of similar tones or values of paints, tinted texture coatings, etc.
- **Frottage techniques** - application of a glaze, followed by partial removal using paper, plastic, fabric or other material to create interesting, organic effects.
- **Metallics and iridescent paints**
- **Fluorescent and phosphorescent paints**
- **Rag-rolling technique** - applying a broken but uniform glaze by using a piece of rag, cloth, cheesecloth, etc down a wall; usually applied on top of a base color or colors.
- **Utilitarian surface bonding*/surface preparation and decorative collage techniques** -(*technique of gluing, bonding or layering of an added material to a hard covered flat surface to improve the appearance and/or minimize prep work needed to fill and sand surface imperfections; such as bonding heavy-duty brown Kraft paper, muslin, or alternate material prior to priming and painting).
- **Stamping and Stenciling**

CHAPTER 11
GALLERY OF ILLUSTRATIONS

PHOTOS & EXAMPLES OF SCENIC PAINTING TECHNIQUES APPLIED TO PRODUCTION

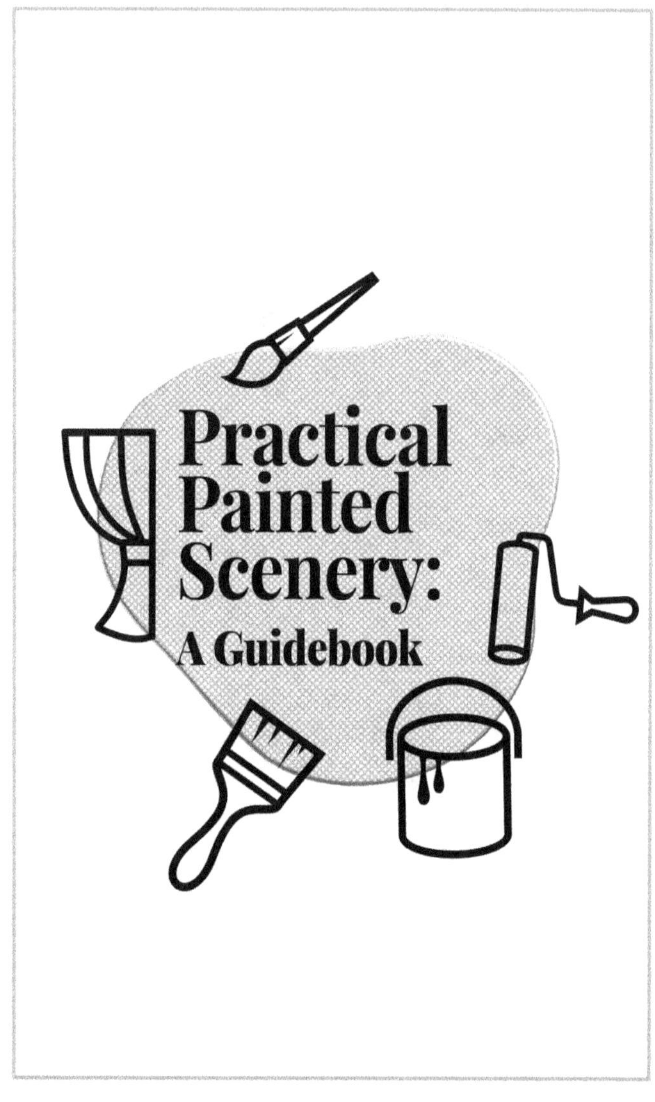
Practical
Painted
Scenery:
A Guidebook

Chapter 1
PLAN & PREP!

Planning & Preparation Makes
For Better Painting

Right: designer drafting & paint elevation. Timothy Jozwick, designer.

Below: drop layout, painting progress, paint elevation. Matthew Baynes, designer.

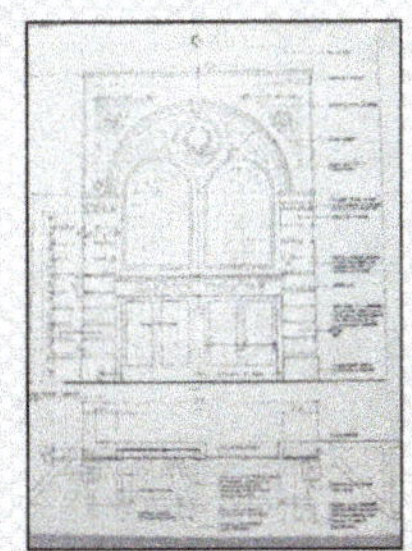
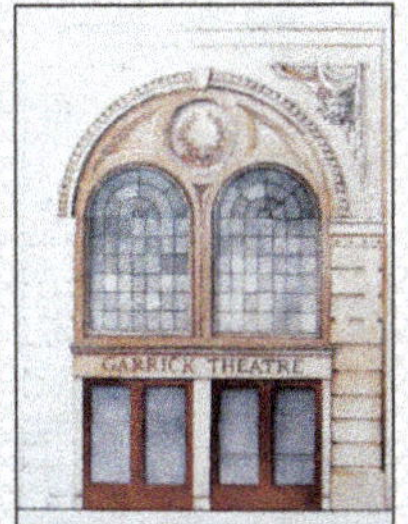

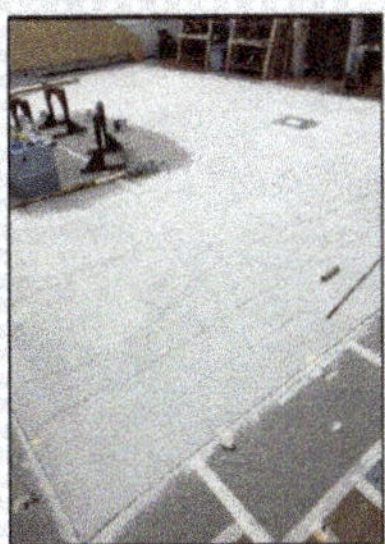
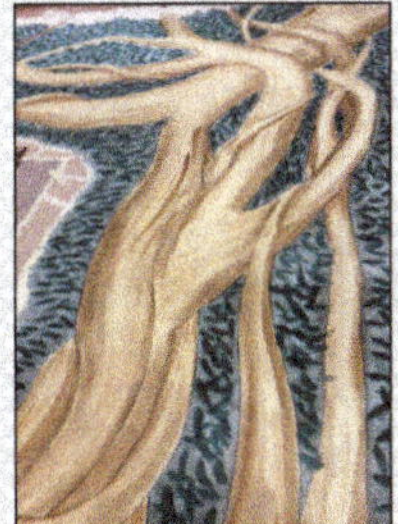
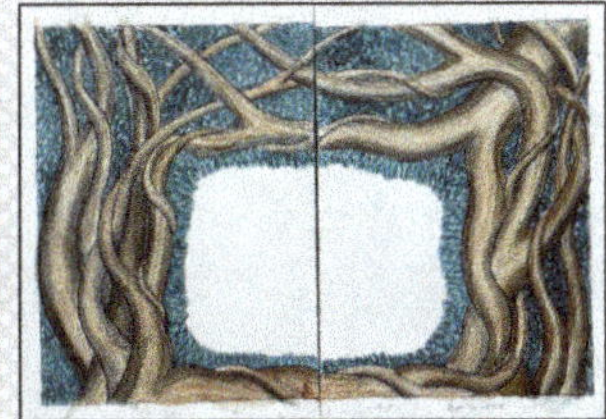

production: _This Girl Laughs, This Girl Cries, This Girl Does Nothing_

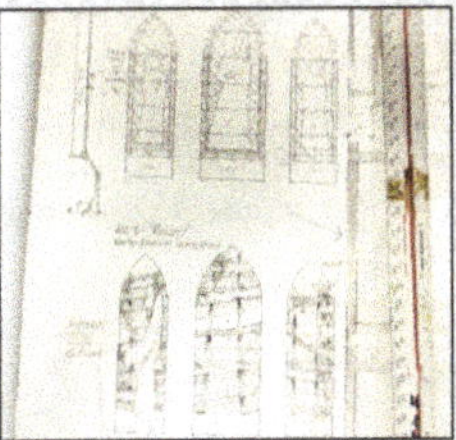
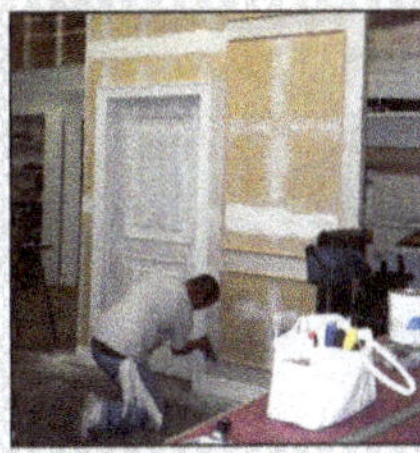
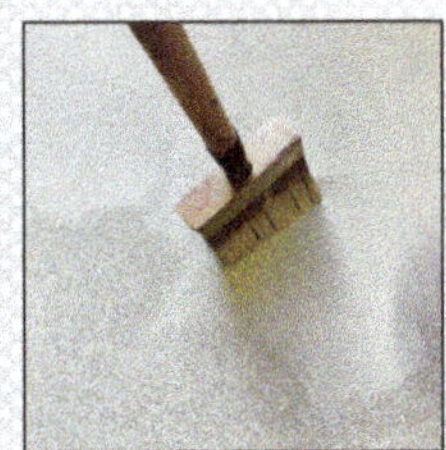

Drawing with scale ruler. Charles McCarry, design

Set painter filling seams and priming hard covered flats

Priming a muslin drop with a large lay-in brush on a pole

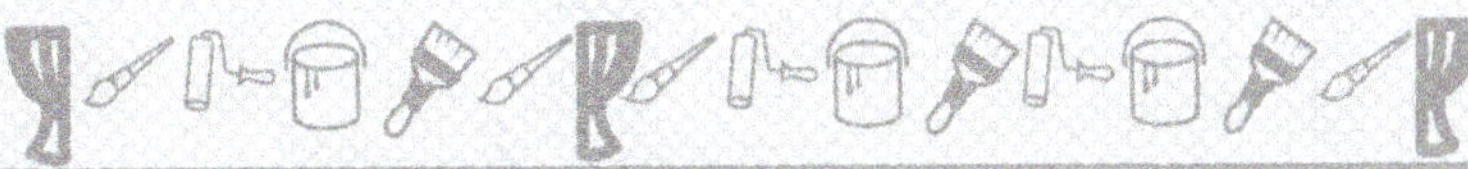

Chapter 2
CHOOSE WISELY!

Paint and Materials Basics

Right: custom mixed washes properly labeled; latex house paints on shelved, in gallon and five gallon containers

Below: interior acrylic house paint; white elastomeric acrylic roof coating

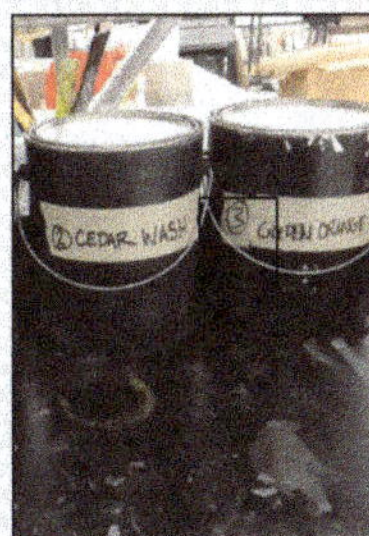

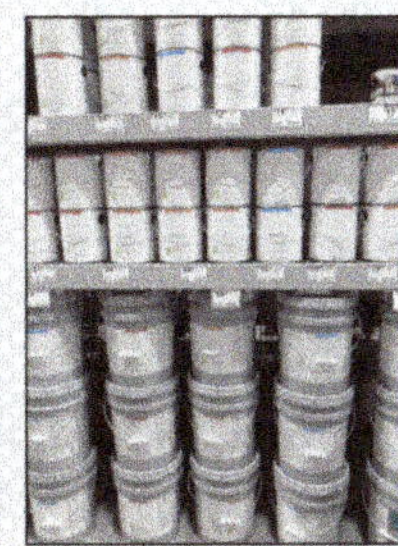

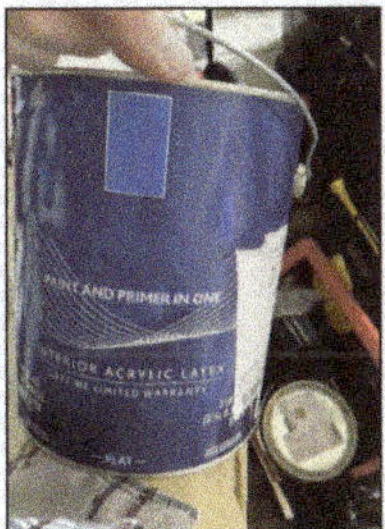

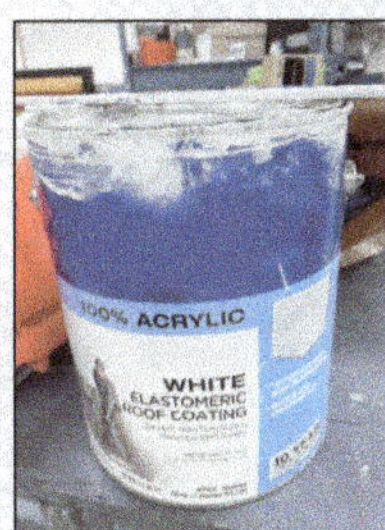

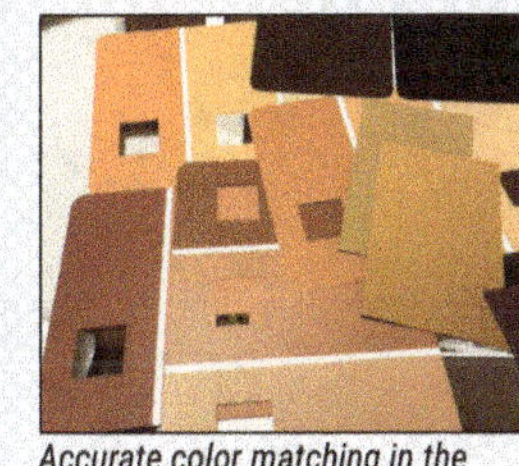

Accurate color matching in the choosing color before product

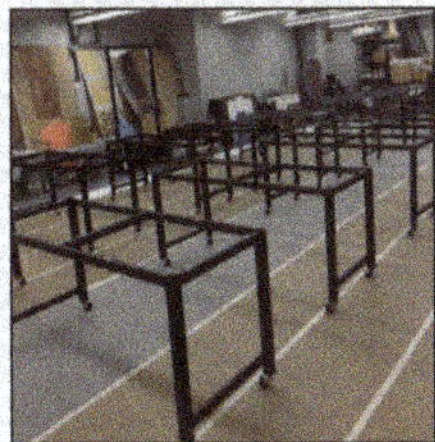

Steel frames in progress, painted with a DTM acrylic

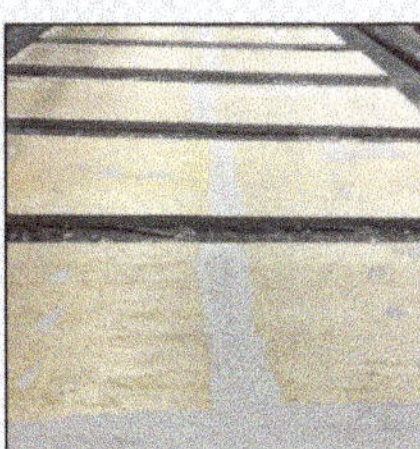

Joint compound used to fill staple holes and seams

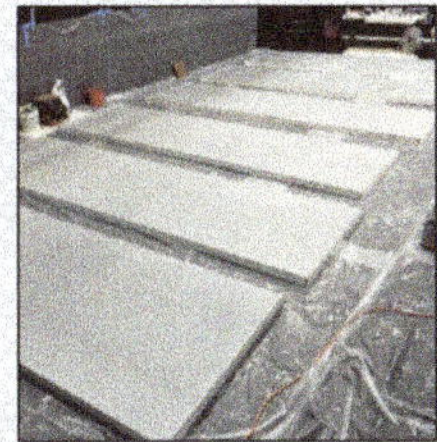

Hard covered flats primed with acrylic latex primer

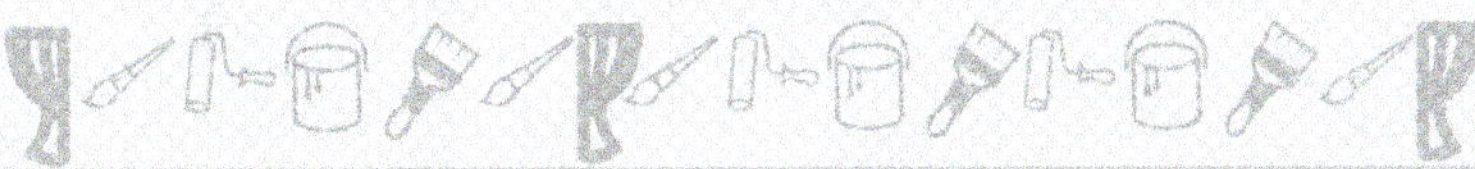

Chapter 3
TOOL TIPS!

Basic Painting Tools Are Best

Right: *paint can opening tools (5-in-one tools, 'church' key); assorted scenic fitches*
Below: *small 'floretta' type sprayer; assorted scenic painting tools, including those used for layout, drawing, paint mixing, prep, wood graining and painting tasks.*

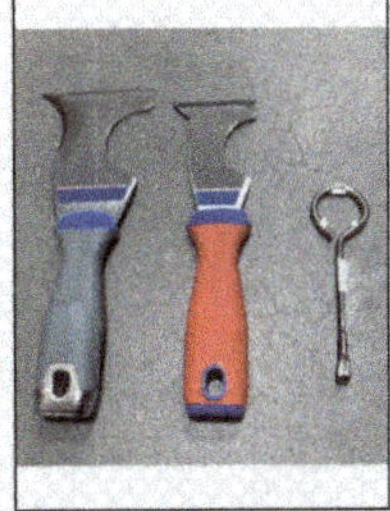

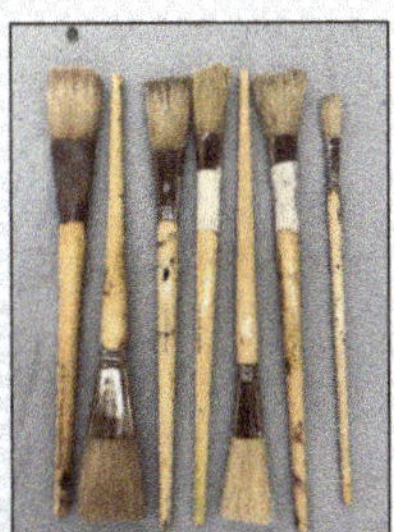

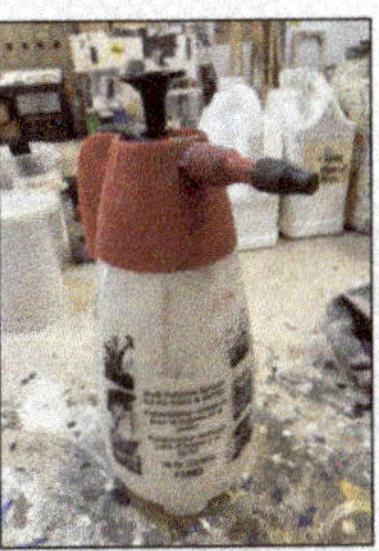

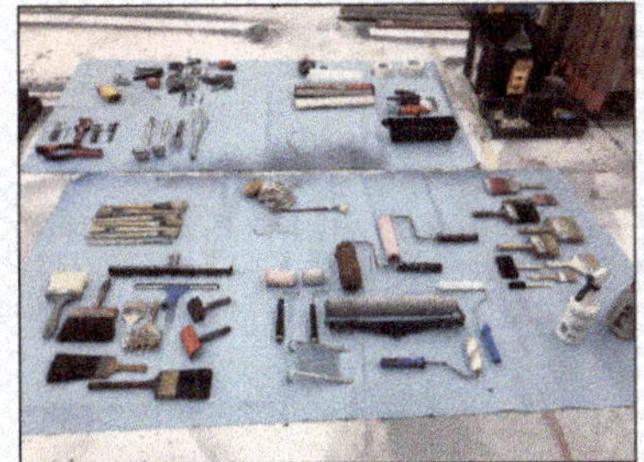

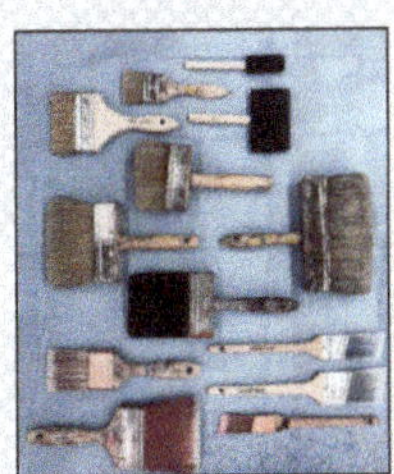

Assortment of commonly used paint brushes

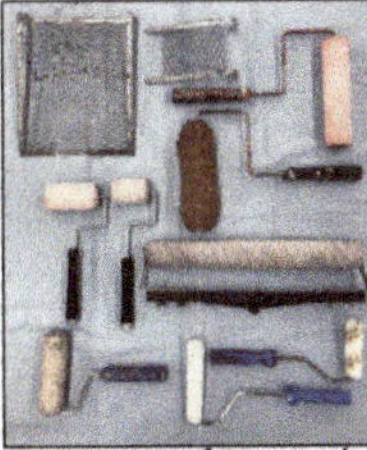

Assortment of commonly used roller frames & grids

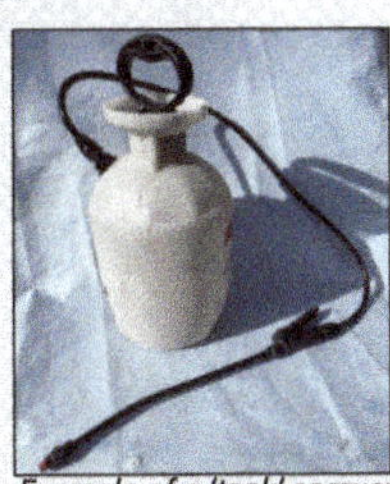

Example of a 'tank' sprayer used for sizing & sprays

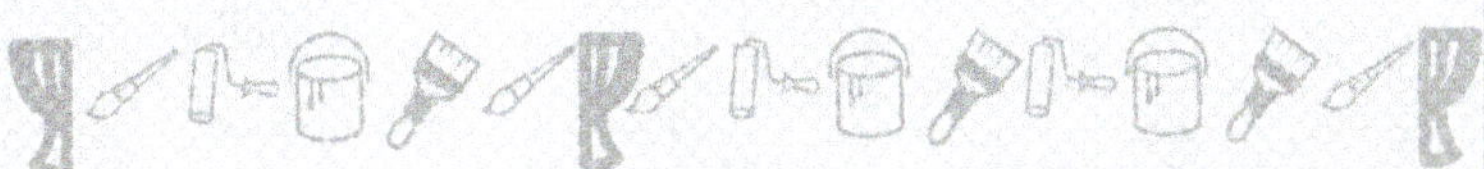

Chapter 4
CUT & ROLL!

Brush and Roller Basics

Right: examples of 'house-painting' brushes with synthetic bristles; standard 9-inch roller frame, cover & roller trays and 18-inch roller frame, cover & roller tray.
Below: examples of 'cut-in' brushwork, rolling a wall, base painting drop with a roller.

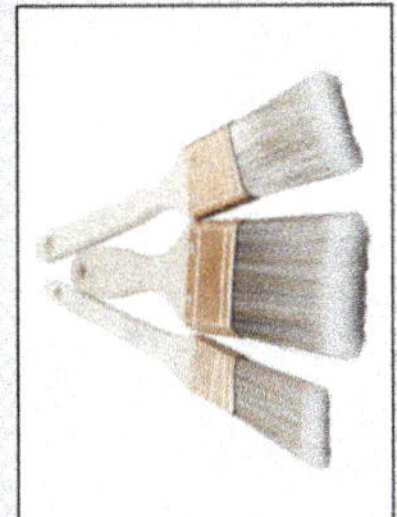

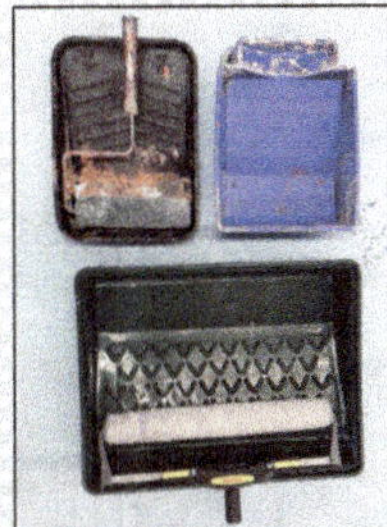

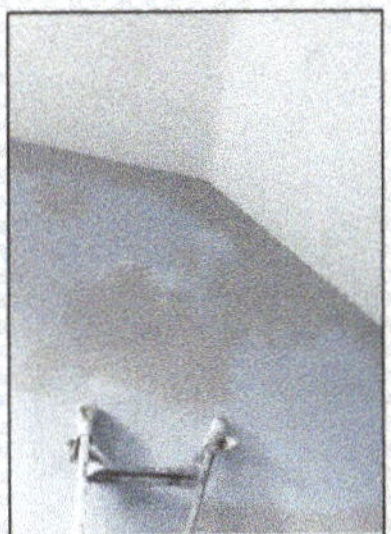

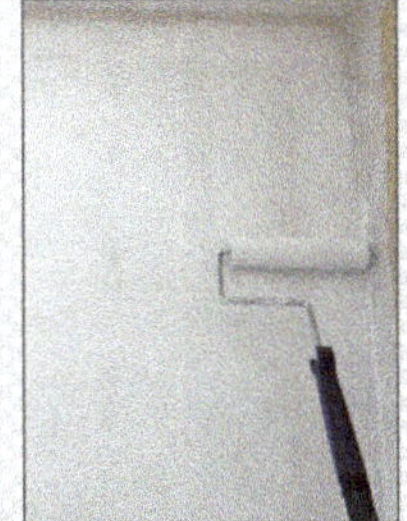

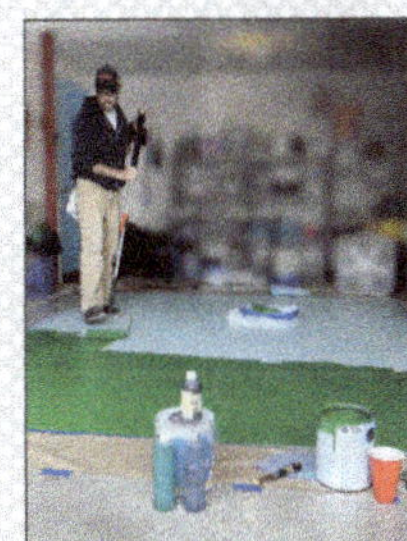

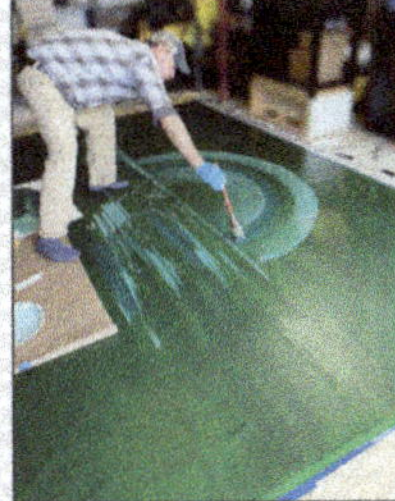

Painting with a scenic fitch on a small backdrop

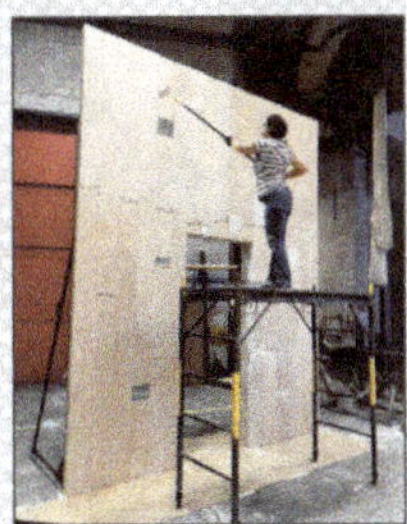

Scenic artist applying primer with a roller

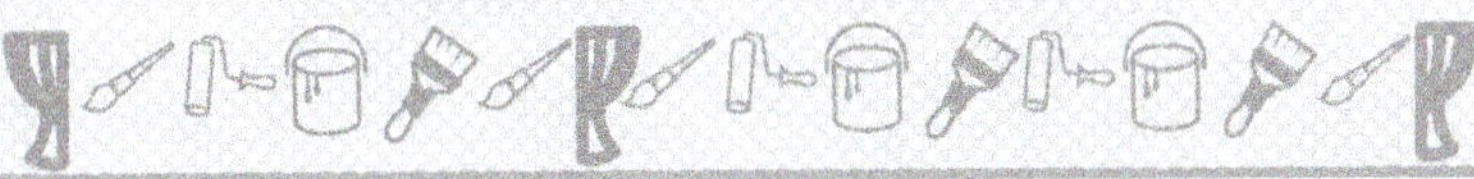

Chapter 5
DRAWING & SCALING 101!

Layout Essentials

Right: drawing with a grid overlay for proportional layout. Timothy Jozwick, designer. String grid in use for cartooning a backdrop. Matthew Baynes, designer.
Below: groundrow layout, and blocking in areas of color. Timothy Jozwick, designer.

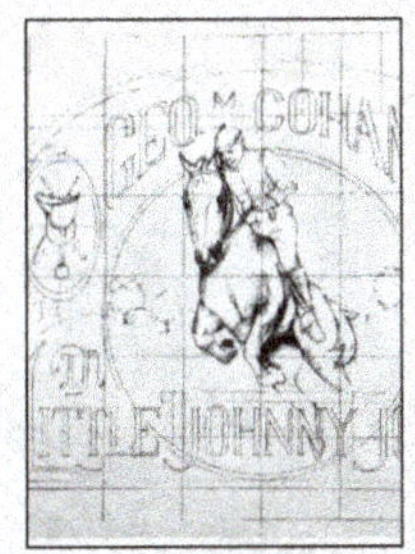

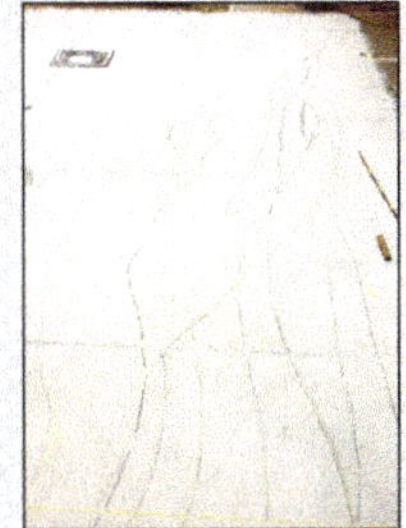

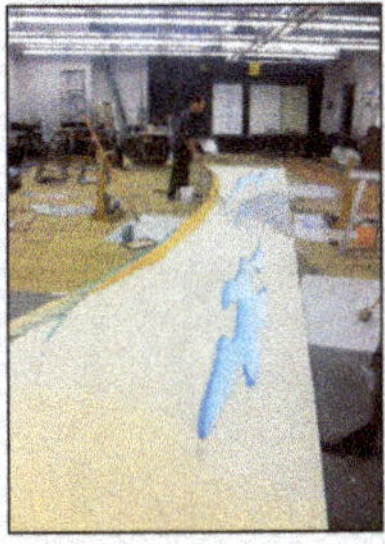

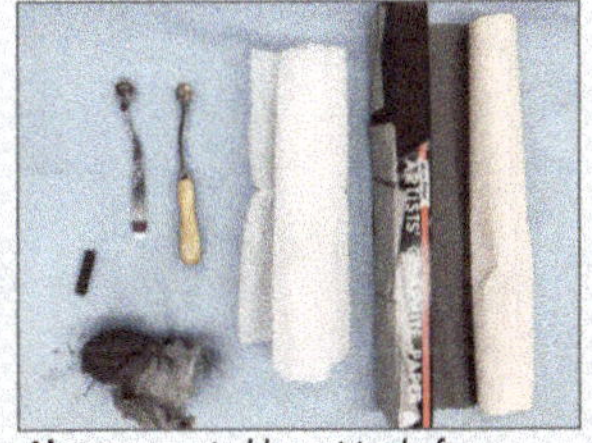

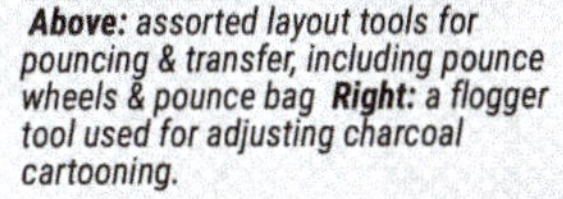

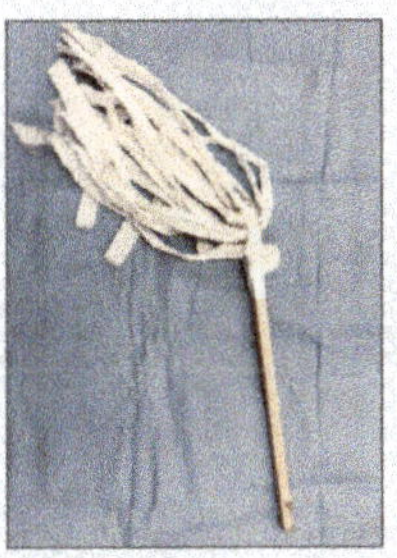

Above: assorted layout tools for pouncing & transfer, including pounce wheels & pounce bag *Right:* a flogger tool used for adjusting charcoal cartooning.

Right: paint elevation for floor. Production: <u>James and the Giant Peach</u>. Timothy Jozwick, designer.

Far Right: scenic artist painting floor. Designer's paint elevation can be seen on stand in center of photograph.

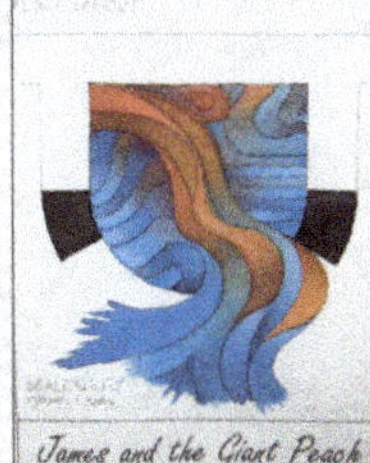

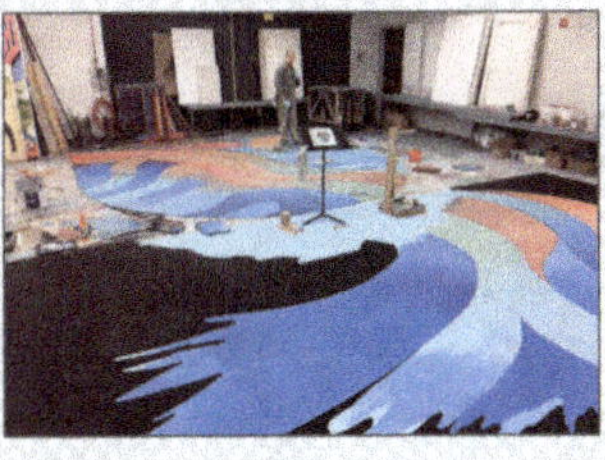

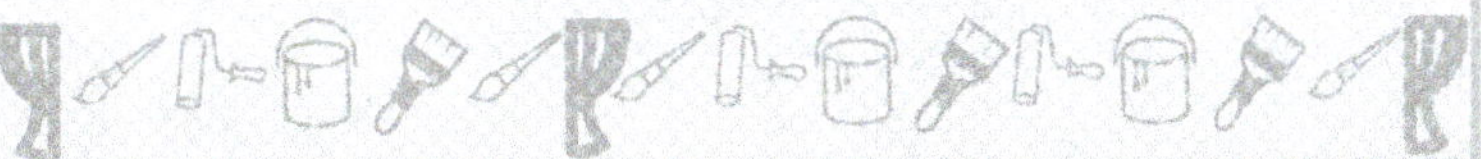

Chapter 6
MIXOLOGY!

Mixing Paint and Working with Color

Right: color wheel illustrating primary colors, complementary colors and locations of tertiary color mixes. *Far Right:* a detailed painted rendition of a Tamara de Lempicka painting. Robert Fetterman-Ojha, scenic artist.

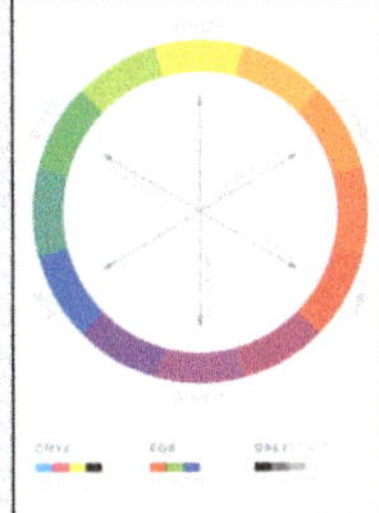

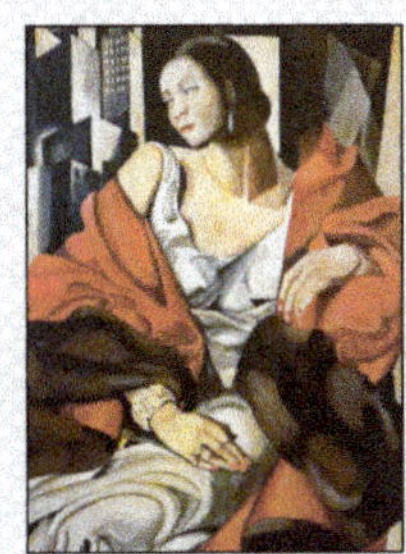

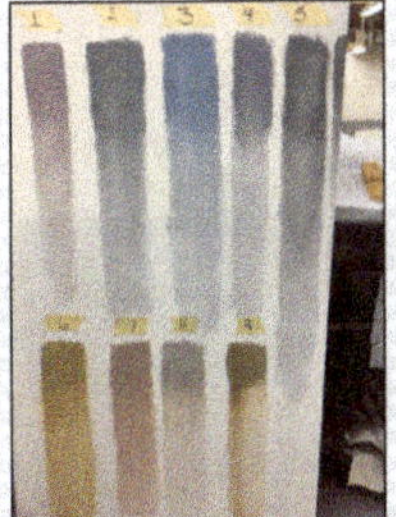

Left: custom mixed palette of colors swatched and labeled in preparation for painting.

Right: hand painted watercolor paint elevation for a backdrop. Brynna Bloomfield, designer. Production: <u>Big Love</u>

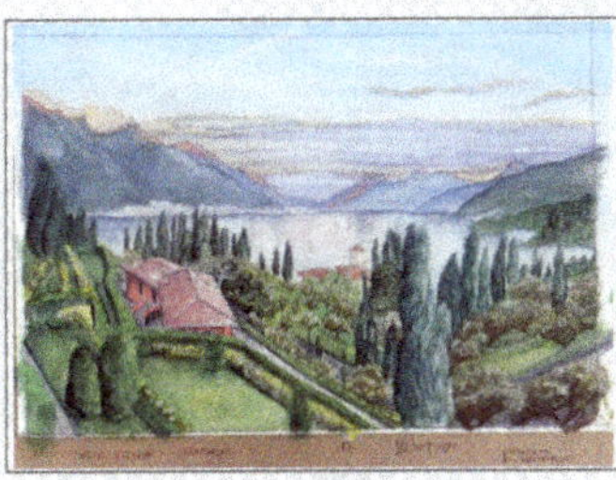

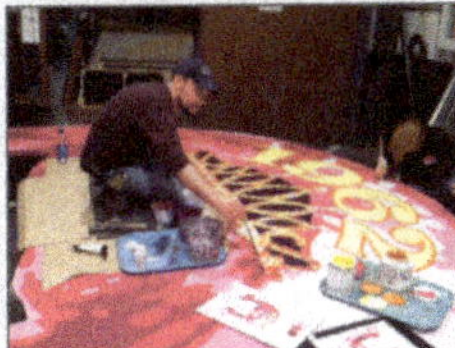

Scenic painters working on a hard-covered flying unit. Joe Keener III, designer. Production: <u>Hairspray</u>

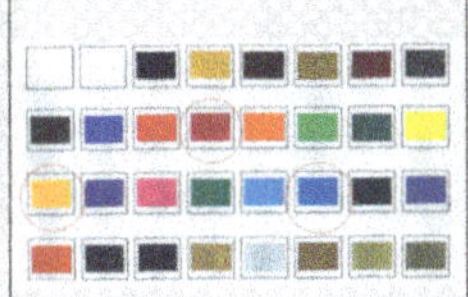

Selection of available scenic paint colors made by Rosco

us.rosco.com

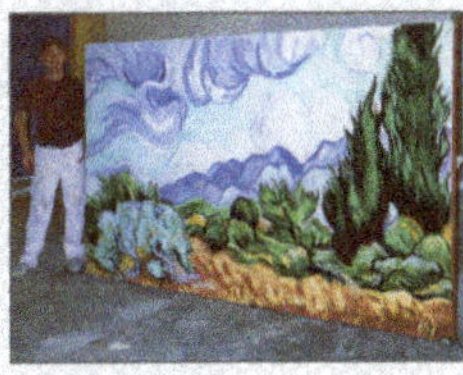

Author with a painted rendition of Van Gogh's Wheat Field with Cypresses (1889)

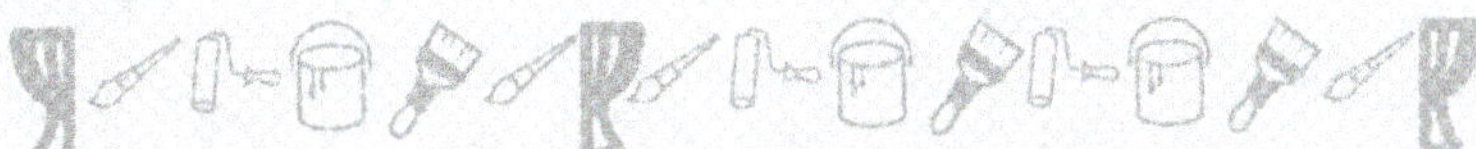

Chapter 7
BETTER WITH TEXTURE!

Texture Coating Application

Right: plaster texture on wall unit; *Far Right:* wall unit with scenic washes and glazes. Cameron Anderson, designer. Production: <u>The Bacchae</u>.
Below: washes, glazes used to accentuate applied texture on faux bricks, brushed scenic 'dope' *(C)*; Cracked paint *(Rt)*.

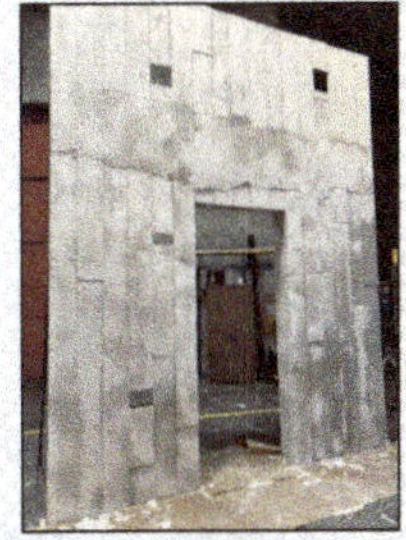

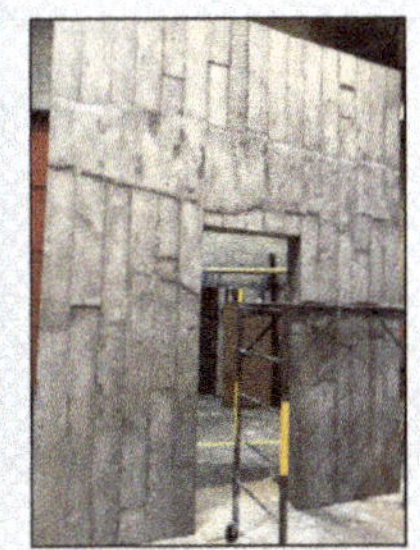

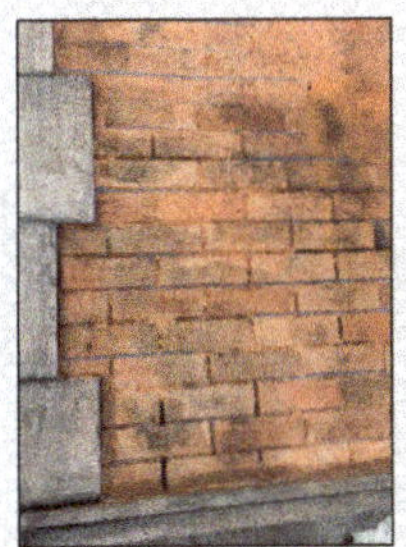

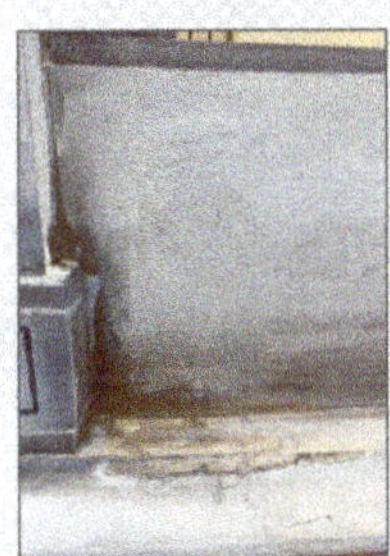

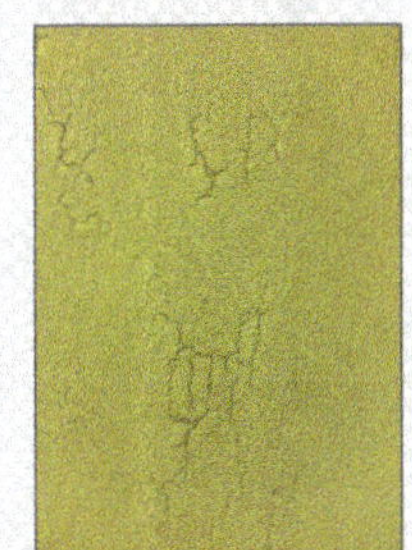

A troweled knockdown finish

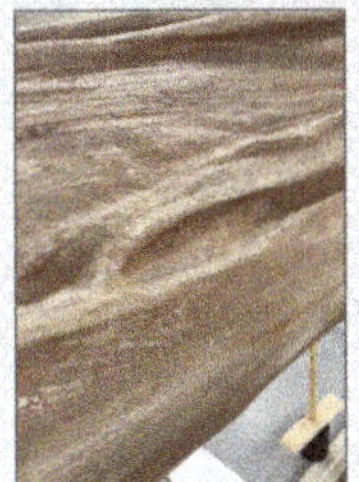

A sculpted and combed faux tree bark

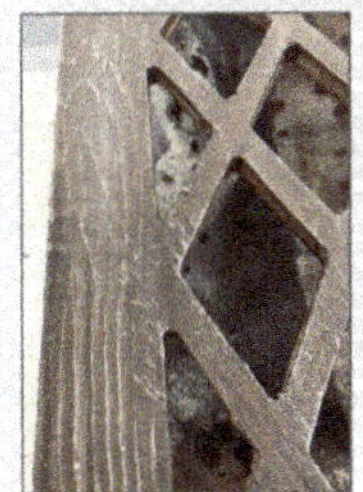

A grain rocker used for creating grain texture

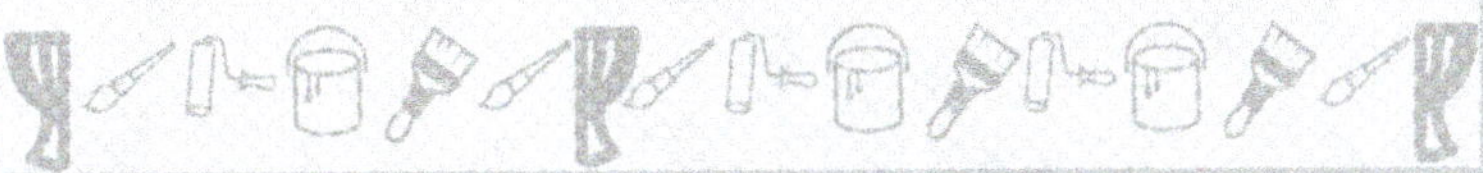

Chapter 8
THINK THIN!

Working with Washes, Sprays and Glazes

Right: typical small hand-held 'floretta' sprayers, along with a funnel and strainer bag used for applying thinned glazes and washes. **Far Right:** a simple wood grain created by pushing a grain glaze across a sealed, glossy base paint color.

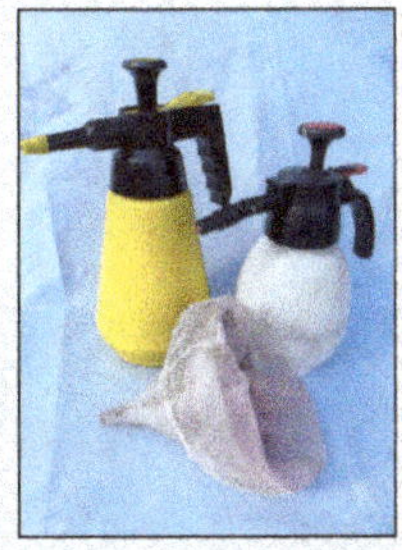
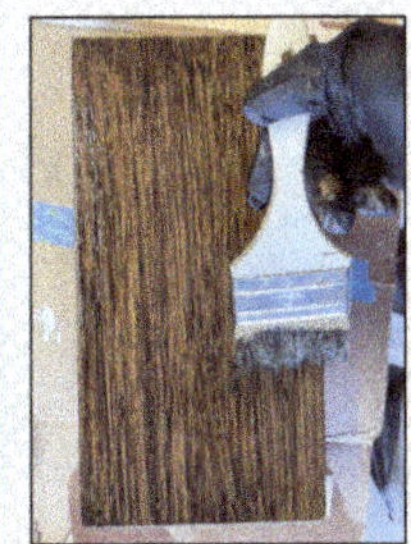

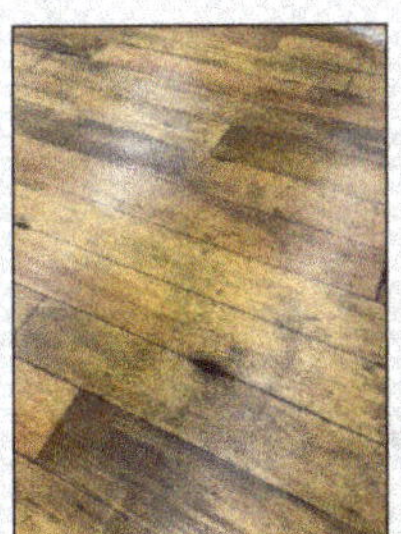

Left: close up view of a spatter and dragged wood-grained painted floor. Ryan Bates, designer.

Right: galaxy panels painted using a combination of sprays applied with a pneumatic gravity feed spray gun and hand spattering. Jane Howland, designer.

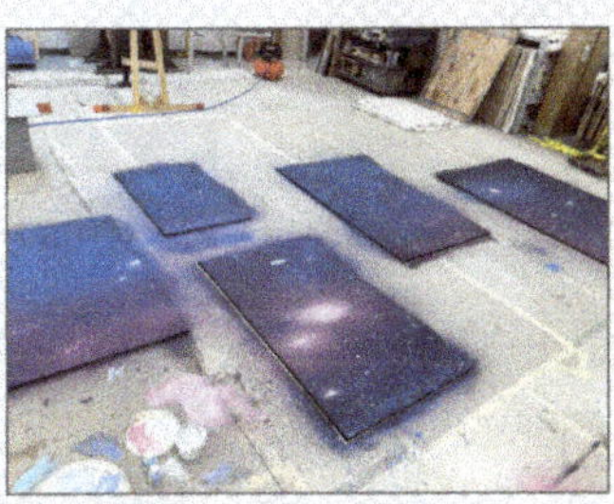

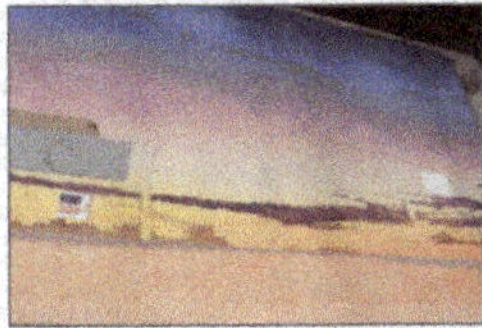

Translucent sprays applied on a painted theatrical backdrop. Sky gradient colors mixed as translucent. Clouds painted as opaque

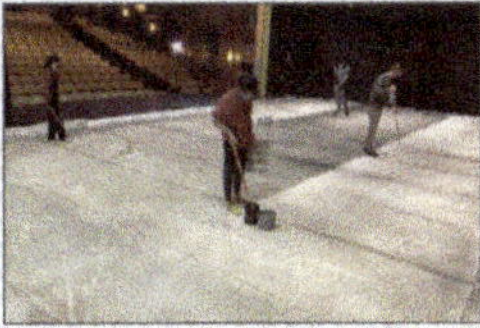

Scenic painters applying thinned paints to translucent scenic gauze panels for a Luciana Stecconi designed production of Into The Woods

Close up example of black paint applied with fine sprays to create an ombré or fade to black at the edges of a painted deck

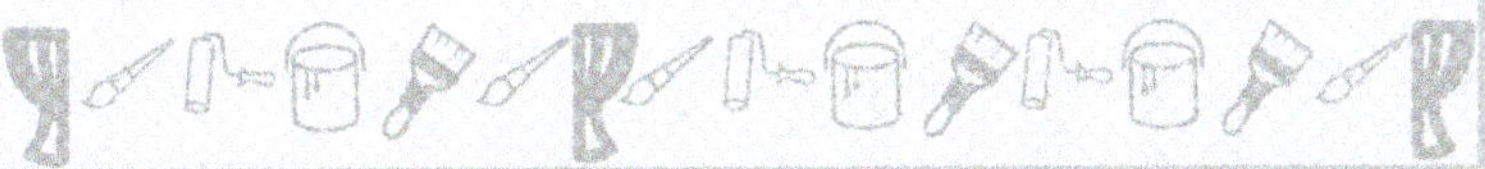

Chapter 9
AGE-OLD 'AGING'!

Techniques for Making New Scenery Look, Well, Not-So-New

Right: peeling-paint and coffee-aging. ***Far Right:*** *Slight frosting effect, rain-age and dirt-aging on plexiglas. Luciana Stecconi, designer. Production: <u>Cabaret</u>.* ***Below:*** *painted, aged broken plaster. Kristen Dempsey, art director. Film: <u>Playland</u> (Dir. Georden West).*

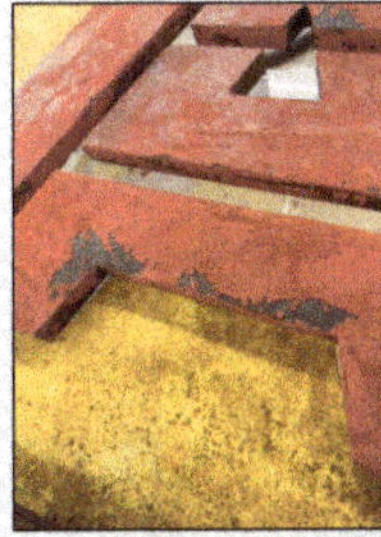

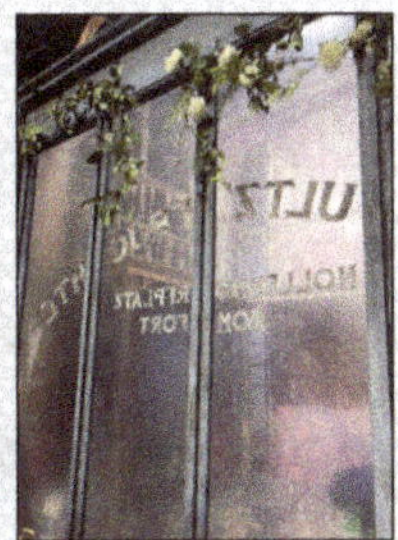

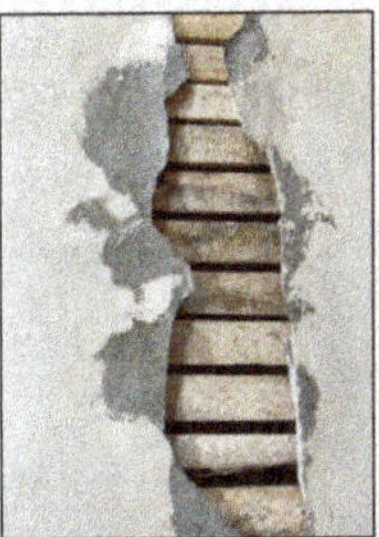

Right: *subtle cracking, tobacco-stain aging on swan backdrop for <u>Playland</u>. Kristen Dempsey, AD.* ***Far Right:*** *distressed, aged vintage wallpaper. Alex Mollo, designer. Production: <u>The Spitfire Grill</u>.*

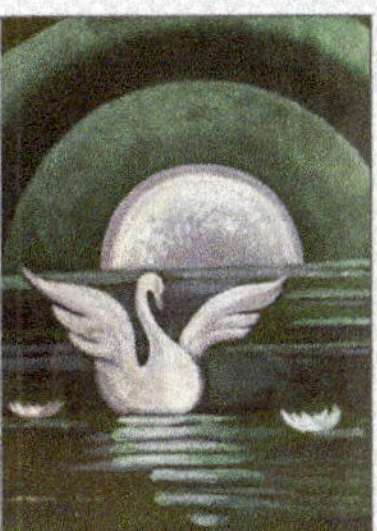

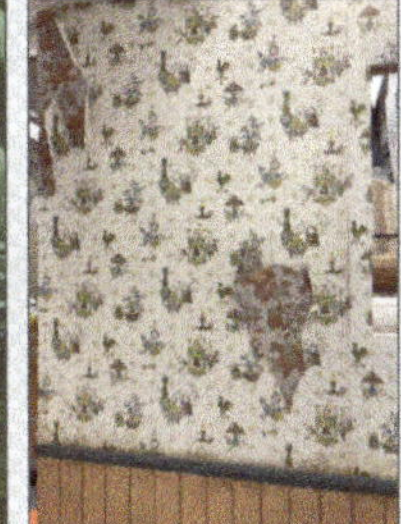

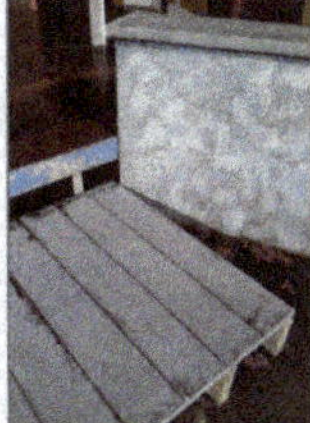

Block-aging, oxidized wood, dirt-aging. Joe Keener III, design

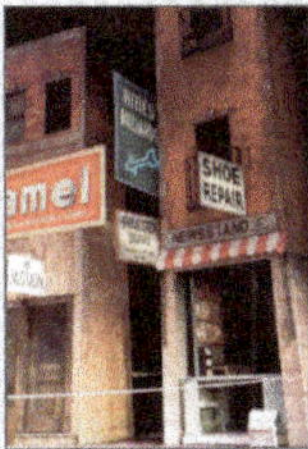

Grunge, rain-aging. Jane Howland, design (<u>Guys & Dolls</u>)

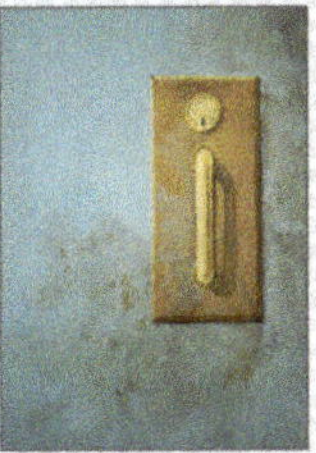

Grunge-aging on trompe l'oeil door handle

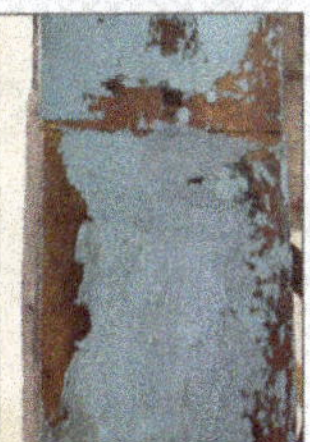

Faux rust, thickened, trowel applied paint for peeling paint effect

Chapter 10
TO SEAL & PROTECT!

Clear Coat Finishes

Right: a popular clear acrylic polyurethane. **Far Right:** application of clear shellac to the front and back of printed paper in preparation for pasting. **Below:** a coating of clear modified oil polyurethane clear finish in a satin finish over painted wood grain.

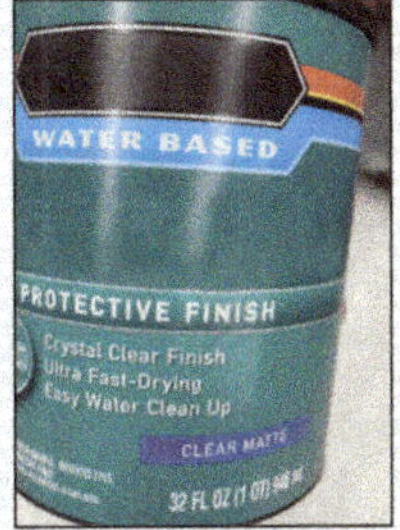

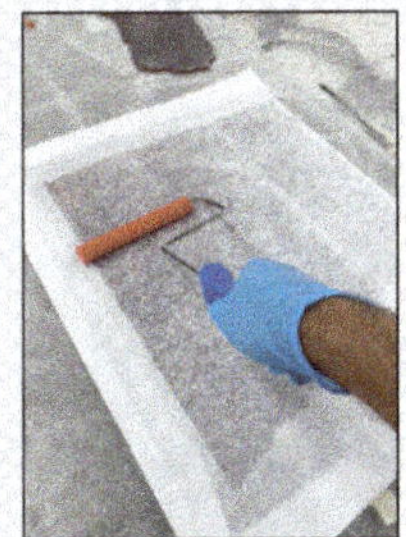

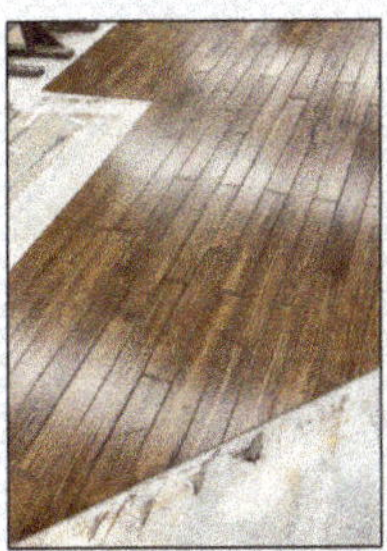

Right: scenic painters apply a final, clear sealer - a water based clear acrylic flat finish - first with a roller, followed by a brushing with a large, soft lay-in brush to eliminate any air bubbles created by the roller cover

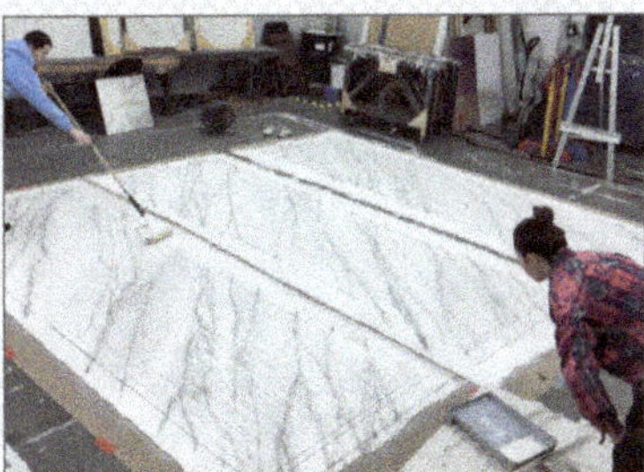

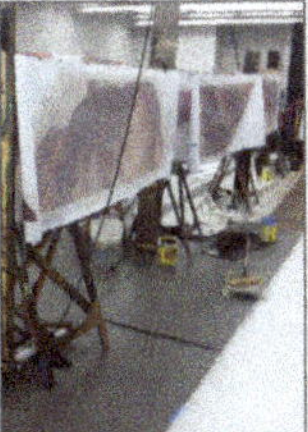

Printed paper, sealed with clear shellac, hanging to dry

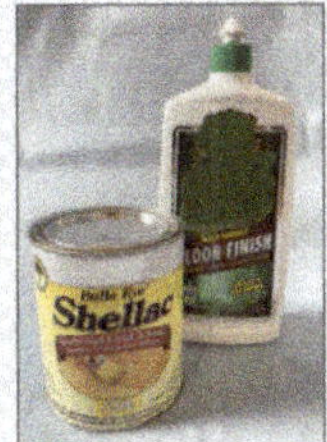

Popular brand of clear shellac; quick-drying floor finish

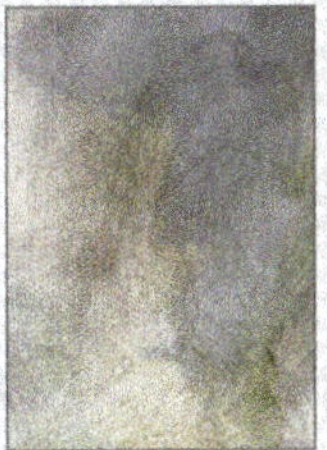

Clear acrylic flat tinted with raw umber pigment for aging

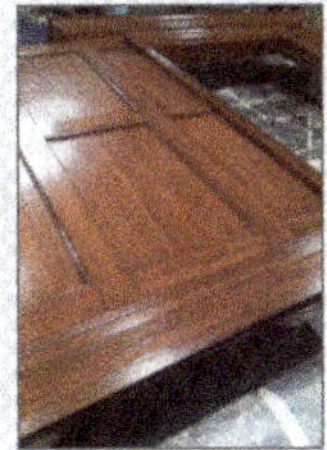

Two coats of clear semi-gloss polyurethane over faux mahogany

ABOUT THE AUTHOR

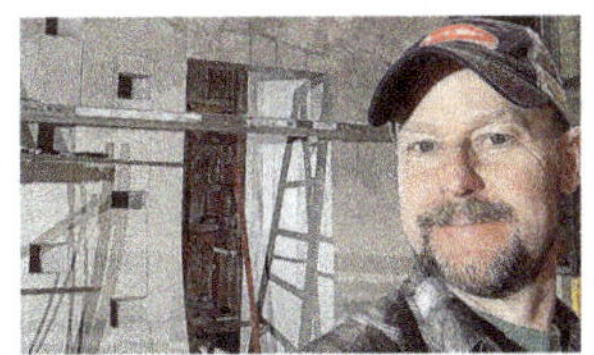

Joe Keener III is a professional scenic painter, designer, educator and author. His painting work has been seen in productions for theater, television, feature films and theme parks in the US, Europe and Japan. Mr. Keener has over 30 years of experience painting, designing and teaching. He is currently the scenic painter for Emerson College and for Emerson Stage, for the Department of Performing Arts, Boston MA.

AFTERWORD & CREDITS
THANKS!

Thank you and credits

This scenic painting guidebook, *Practical Painted Scenery: A Guidebook*, would not be possible without the efforts and support of the following individuals, who it is important to mention. Many thanks to each of you!

- To Elizabeth Nunnery (enthusiasm to assist on this Guidebook, along with your graphics and editorial work).
- To my fellow Emerson College & Emerson Stage colleagues (both current and former): David Colfer, Timothey Sullivan, Maureen Shea, Melia Bensussen, Scott Pinkney, Robert Colby, Amelia Broome, Luciana Stecconi, Keith Cornelius, Timothy Jozwick, Kristin Knutson, Ryan Bates, Connor Thompson, Sarah Spollett, Richelle Devereaux-Murray, Laurie Bramhall; painting students and painting staff, who design and practice these painting techniques - showing, enlightening and learning as we strive together to make every painted unit as good as we can.

- To the many mentors/designers/painters, who I have been both fortunate & grateful to learn from, to paint alongside, and to count among my friends - many have graciously provided wonderful examples of their scenic design and scenic painting work here* and for the *Scenic Compendium*: Robert Fetterman-Ojha*, Timothy Jozwick*, Michael Brewer*, Charles McCarry*, Luciana Stecconi*, Brynna Bloomfield*, Jane Howland*, Matthew Baynes*, Cameron Anderson*, Kristen Dempsey*, Alex Mollo*, Patrick Lynch, Daniela Weiser, Peter Durand, Larry Shepard, Christopher Holcombe, Bob Brookman, David Newell, David Park, Bil Volker, Barbara Rama, Anthony Siakiewicz, William Walmsley.. and so many others!
- To all of my family; including Bonnie & Bee.
- For Franciane, for consistent encouragement and support, with love.

If you enjoyed reading this book and found it to be useful and/or interesting, please take a moment to leave a brief comment or recommendation. You can support this author and encourage more content in the near future. Thank you for reading!

INDEX

ALSO BY JOE E. KEENER III

25@52: Collected Poems

The Myth of Seashells: Collected Poems

Is Bee a Roo? story by Fran Royer, drawings by Joe Keener III

Scenic Compendium: Techniques, Tools & Tricks for Theatrical Scenic Painting (with Emily Curtis)